GROW IN GRACE

GROW IN GRACE

Sinclair B. Ferguson

Marshalls

Marshalls Paperbacks
Marshall Morgan & Scott

1 Bath Street, London EC1V 9LB

First published by Marshall Morgan & Scott 1981

ISBN 0 551 00922 5

Photoset in Great Britain by
Rowland Phototypesetting Ltd
Bury St Edmunds, Suffolk
Printed in Great Britain by
Hunt Barnard Printing Ltd
Aylesbury, Bucks

To
Eric J. Wright
who has helped many
to **Grow in Grace**

Contents

Introduction

Grow in Grace is a book about the way we develop and mature as Christians.

When a baby is born there is great rejoicing. Parents are relieved to discover that the little one is well, and they are delighted by the miracle of new life. But every parent knows that birth is only the beginning. Every baby must grow. Food, warmth, affection and exercise will all be necessary in the years which lie ahead. The baby will begin to crawl, then walk and run. Its knowledge will increase, its personality develop as it responds to the circumstances and experiences of life. The marriage of natural characteristics with life-experiences will produce a unique person. There will be opportunities to take, obstacles to overcome before maturity is reached.

So it is in the Christian life as well. If we are to grow in grace we need spiritual nourishment, protection, exercise and knowledge. Only through these means will we ever become the kind of Christian men and women God intends us to be. *Grow in Grace* has been written to help you to understand how God's intentions can be fulfilled in your own experience.

Some books on Christian living and growing might best be described as 'how-to' books. They present a kind of 'do-it-yourself' manual for Christian living, and explain the mechanics of Bible-reading, prayer, Christian service and so on. You can find helpful counsel in such books. But *Grow in Grace* is not that kind of book. The difference is not accidental. In a sense it is intended to reflect the principle which Paul explained to the Corinthians: Paul may plant, Apollos may water, *but God makes things grow* (1 Cor. 3:6–7). At the end of the day, while there is much we can do to encourage growth in ourselves and each other, true spiritual development is something which God himself gives.

This, then, is the emphasis of these chapters. At many points they provide or suggest instruction about what we must do in order to grow. But their main underlying thrust is this: our greatest need is to recognise, and to put our lives under, the influences which God uses to produce growth in Christian character. If we can learn some of the principles he employs—that is, if we become familiar with those ways and thoughts of God which are always higher than our own (Is. 55:8–9)—we will be more likely to advance steadily in the Christian life. That is why I have combined exposition of biblical principles with their illustrated application in the lives of some of the great biblical characters. This is what Scripture itself does—or so it seems to me—and we are always on safe ground when we follow its example and try to capture its spirit.

I am grateful to John Hunt of Marshall Morgan and Scott who suggested the theme of this book to me. Without his suggestion and encouragement it would not have been written. I am also profoundly grateful to my wife Dorothy, and to our children, David, Peter, John and Ruth. They provide the family context in which I seek to grow in grace, and they have all done their very best to help me to write about it!

SINCLAIR B. FERGUSON
GLASGOW, JULY 1981

10

SECTION ONE
CHRIST OUR LIFE

The whole of the Christian life is centred on Jesus Christ. Like Paul the contemporary Christian can say: 'To me to live is Christ'.

But often, in Christian experience, we are tempted to look elsewhere for direction, example, counsel and guidance. We lose sight of the fact that everything we need to live the Christian life is to be found exclusively in Jesus.

For this reason when we begin thinking about spiritual growth as well we must think first of all about Jesus.

1: Jesus—The Pioneer

We were born in order to grow. When someone becomes a Christian the transformation which takes place in them is called 'the new birth'. They have been 'born again' (Jn. 3:3,5). Like new born babies they *see* the kingdom of God, they cry 'Abba, Father', and they need milk in order to grow. (So we are taught by Jesus, Jn. 3:3; Paul, Rom. 8:15, and Peter, 1 Pet. 2:2.)

What happens when we grow? One of the things which often happens in natural life is that we become more like our parents! At first, when we are babies, people will ask 'Who is he like?' 'Is she like her mum?' Later in life, when they have not seen us for a period of time, they will exclaim (to our embarrassment!) 'My, how like your mother you are!' We may feel that we have left behind us the influence of our parents, only to discover—perhaps in a crisis—that the old family characteristics remain with us for the rest of our lives.

The writers of the New Testament were often struck by the fact that this principle is equally true of the Christian life. One of the things which should begin to happen to the child of God is that he or she should grow up to resemble the character and to reproduce the actions of a heavenly Father. That is why Jesus' commandment was that we should be perfect, just as our Father in heaven is perfect (Mt. 5:48).

But, there is another common characteristic of

family life. Children in the same family resemble each other. We are often asked about our children: 'Is he like David?', 'Is she like Peter' and from time to time we notice striking similarities. People expect that younger brothers and sisters will have the same features as an elder brother.

As Christians we too have an elder brother. Jesus is described as 'the firstborn among many brothers' (Rom. 8:29). The New Testament tells us that God's plan is to make all his children like his Son Jesus.

For all practical purposes the message of the New Testament could be summarised in these words: God wants us to be his own children; he wants us to share the family-likeness. He is working in our lives in order to make us like Jesus. He wants us too to shape our lives so that they will be like Jesus.

There is nothing more important to learn about Christian growth than this: *Growing in grace means becoming like Jesus*.

The significance of this is so fundamental that it is worth spelling out in greater detail what it means:

JESUS, who grew in grace himself, IS THE SOURCE OF SPIRITUAL GROWTH
JESUS, who grew in grace himself, IS THE EXAMPLE OF SPIRITUAL GROWTH
JESUS WAS A MAN HIMSELF, THAT IS WHY HE TOO NEEDED TO GROW SPIRITUALLY.

Why are these statements so important? For two reasons. They are often either *denied* or they are *exaggerated*.

They are *exaggerated* when people think of

Jesus as no more than a man—as a good and great teacher, perhaps even as a miracle worker or someone sent by God. When we suggest that Jesus was only a man the whole of the Christian gospel begins to disintegrate and crumble. For if Jesus is only to be thought of as a man, many of his claims, much of his teaching, the confessions of the early Christians and the claims they made for him, all amount to nothing. Indeed, Jesus could not have been a good man, or a great teacher if his claim to a unique relationship with God proves false.

But there is also the danger that Christians may *deny* that Jesus was truly and fully man. Many people who have believed in Jesus' divinity, the fact that he is God, have found it difficult to accept that he really shared our human nature. They have difficulty in believing (and *feeling*) that Jesus entered fully into our experience.

Why is that such a crucial matter? If you think about it, you will realise that we have already suggested the answer.

Being a Christian, growing in grace, means becoming like Jesus. But if we are modelling our lives on a Jesus who was not really human, who did not really get inside our experiences, we will end up living Christian lives which are lacking in the warmth and compassion of real humanity. It is just as well that we should realise that there are many Christians just like that. We are all ashamed of it, but it is true. Some Christians do seem to have rather steely glints in their eyes. They are not like the Jesus of whom you read in the Gospels. It is not because they lack earnestness, or prayer, or zeal. It is because they are living their Christian lives on the basis of a wrong design.

Have you ever made something from a pattern

or design? You may have built a model, or knitted a jersey. Have you ever been totally frustrated when everything has gone wrong, only to discover that you have been following the wrong page in the instructions or the pattern? How frustrated you were! Exactly the same happens in the lives of some Christians because they never look carefully at the pattern which the Bible gives us in Jesus. But a Christianity which does not produce true humanity in our lives is surely a fraudulent version of the message and life of Jesus. That is why it is so fundamental for us to see that in spiritual growth we begin by recognising that Jesus our Saviour grew. He is our example.

> *Teach me how to grow in goodness*
> *Daily as I grow;*
> *Thou hast been a child, and surely*
> *Thou dost know.*

W. J. Mathams

THE FACT OF JESUS' GROWTH

Luke, who wrote the third Gospel, was a doctor. He seems to have been one of the most educated of the early Christians. He was also interested in things which did not attract the attention of the other Gospel writers. He tells us at the beginning of the Gospel that he had done a good deal of study on the life of Jesus. What he offers to us is an account which has been carefully researched and includes the testimony of eye witnesses (Lk. 1:1–3).

One of these eye witnesses was, in all likelihood, Mary the mother of Jesus. The Gospel opens with two long chapters which could probably have come from no other source. Luke even seems to hint at this when he tells us at the end of chapter two how Mary 'treasured all these things in her heart' (Lk. 2:51).

What did Mary remember? Like every mother she recalled the stages of Jesus' development.

The Jews divided a child's growth into eight different stages from birth through to adulthood. Luke reduces these stages to three, which read like a chorus running through Mary's account of the life of this wonderful child born and brought up in her home:

The child grew and became strong in spirit (Lk. 1:80)

The child grew and became strong; he was filled with wisdom and the grace of God was upon him (Lk. 2:40)

Jesus grew in wisdom and stature, and in favour with God and man (Lk. 2:52)

Two things went side by side with Jesus. He grew physically. His body developed and became stronger. As we read between the lines in the Gospels we learn why. He was a country boy. He revelled in the outdoor life. The birds, the animals, the sea, the whole world of nature coloured his way of explaining the spiritual world. It is so obvious from his teaching that like most other boys he just loved being outside, walking, running, playing. He was also Joseph's apprentice. He worked with his hands, carried wood for yokes on his shoulders, and tested them on oxen to see whether they were 'easy' (Matt. 11:28–30). No wonder he grew strong!

Mary noticed something else about Jesus. She could not avoid recognising it, even in a member of her own family. He grew strong in spirit. He was filled with wisdom. The grace of God was upon his life. In her own home lived a boy, a teenager, then a fully grown man about whom she could say: 'He grew in favour with God'. Here is clear proof for our earlier statement that JESUS HIMSELF GREW IN GRACE.

We need to be very clear what this does not mean. It does not mean that the Lord Jesus was morally imperfect and therefore needed to grow to perfection. He was perfect at every stage of his life. He was without sin as a child, and he maintained his sinlessness until the end of his life.

But our Lord, our example, was a perfect *man*. He grew through every stage of his life, in understanding and capacity. As his natural powers grew, so he was constantly faced with the challenge of submitting them to God and the temptation to use them for other self-seeking ends. The obedience he gave to God as a seven year old boy was as perfect as the obedience he showed when he willingly died on the cross and suffered terrible torments in order to fulfil his Father's will. But his obedience on the cross, while no more perfect, was far, far greater than the kind of obedience which was appropriate to his life as a boy. This is what Luke means when he says that even as a young boy Jesus' spiritual growth could be seen, and what Paul means when he says that Jesus' obedience reached its height on the cross when he became obedient even to the point of dying (Phil. 2:8).

Because of this growth in grace and obedience, Jesus grew in favour with God. The more he obeyed his Father, the more cause his Father had to love him. Of course the Father has always loved his only Son. But perfect love can always respond to new experiences and to new reasons for expressing itself. The 'perfect' love which a newly engaged couple share together is still capable of reaching new depths of fulness when they are married. They will find new reasons for love. Similarly Jesus himself said that the Father loved him because he was *going to lay down his life* (Jn. 10:17). Because he obeyed God to the limit as man, his Father's love for him knew no bounds. As Jesus grew in obedience it was natural that he should also grow in the favour of his Father.

But what exactly was involved in the growth of Jesus? What is the meaning of it?

THE SIGNIFICANCE OF JESUS' GROWTH

Luke says Jesus grew. The word he uses has an interesting and illuminating background. Originally it meant 'making one's way forward by pushing aside obstacles'. It was a nautical and military metaphor. A ship sailing to its destination would make its way through hazards and difficulties on the high seas. An army, marching through rough terrain might have to hack its way through a forest, or overcome the difficulties of a river in spate. Later on the word came to have the much less picturesque meaning of making progress of any kind. It may have that mundane meaning here. But it is certainly very helpful and encouraging to think of Jesus in the context of its original meaning.

When we say that Jesus grew spiritually and therefore is able to help us to grow spiritually, what do we mean? We mean that, just as we find there are obstacles in our way, things were no different for Jesus. Just as there are pressures on us to give way and live lives of less than whole-hearted obedience to God, he too felt these pressures. He lived in 'the likeness of sinful flesh' (Rom. 8:3); he experienced weakness, hunger, thirst, fear, opposition of all kinds just as we do. Jesus lived his life in *our* world.

The Gospel writers underline the fact that Jesus did not come to the Garden of Eden, but to a broken fallen world to be a Saviour and Example for his disciples. Although he was the Second Man and the Last Adam (cf. 1 Cor. 15:45, 47) he came to be tempted not in a garden but a desert. He was tested when he was hungry. He was not surrounded by a tame creation, but by wild beasts (Lk. 4:1–2; Mk. 1:12–13). Jesus had to hack his way through the jungle which our sin had created in order to grow in his obedience to his Father in heaven.

This is one of the reasons why Jesus is given the title *Archēgos* by the early Christians. The word *Archēgos* does not have a one word equivalent in English. It means someone who leads, and by his leadership stirs others into activity and brings them with him. It was used in classical Greek of the heroes who founded great cities. Perhaps if in those far-off days schools had 'Founder's Day' this was the word which was used. The Founder of a school is not only the person who began it. He is the person whose example is meant to serve as a model and stimulus to the pupils in years to come.

Jesus, says Peter, is the *Archēgos* of life (Acts 3:15). He was the first to be resurrected from the dead, *and* he is the one whose resurrection causes our resurrections (1 Cor. 15:20–3). Hebrews tells us that Jesus is the Author (*Archēgos*) and the Pioneer (*Archēgos*) of our faith and salvation

(Heb. 2:10; 12:2). He is the great trail-blazer.

Picture an army captain hacking his way through a jungle during a battle with guerilla forces. He leads his men from danger to safety by first facing the dangers, impediments and tests himself. Similarly Jesus is the Captain of our salvation. He has tasted all of our experiences of temptation. He has gone further. He has experienced them in their full strength, when they have unleashed all their powers against him. Where we would stumble and fall, he has pressed on. He overcame temptation, conquered death and drew its sting. Now he beckons to us: 'Follow me, men; the pathway of faith is safe for all of you to use!'

When the New Testament speaks about the fulness of grace which we find in Christ, it does not mean only forgiveness, pardon and justification. Christ has done much more for us. He died for us. But he also *lived* for us, so that we might draw on his strength. He grew in grace, and when we draw on his power we shall likewise grow in grace.

It is a constant principle that faith can only receive what grace provides and can only believe what Scripture reveals. But faith should receive everything grace provides and Scripture reveals. We tend to impoverish our spiritual experience and deny ourselves the help of Christ when we fail to see how important his spiritual growth was. But when we see that our Saviour was one who himself grew in grace, new dimensions of his love for us, new possibilities of our own spiritual development are opened to us.

The Christian life depends on how we think about Jesus. Do you think of him as the author, the pioneer of spiritual growth?

2: How Jesus Grew

In chapter one we began to think about the *fact* of Jesus Christ's spiritual growth. Now we must look at this in more detail. How did this work out in practice?

One of the ways in which we can do this is by mapping out from our Lord's life some of the key features of his own experience in which he blazes a trail for us to follow. It is because he has experienced what we experience that he is able to see us through in our struggles towards spiritual growth (Heb. 2:18; 4:15–16). What were the ways in which his Father brought Jesus to spiritual maturity?

THE PATTERN OF JESUS' OWN GROWTH

When we read the New Testament with this question in mind, there seem to be at least four different ways in which we can think of his personal growth as a servant of God.

1. *He grew in the fruit of the Spirit.* When Paul describes the fruit of God's Spirit in the life of the Christian in Galatians 5:22–3 he is of course giving us a picture of Jesus. He was the one who was baptised with the Spirit and experienced him without limitation (Jn. 2:34).

It makes a thrilling Bible study to examine Paul's list of Spirit-grown qualities and trace each of them through the life and ministry of our Lord. See his *love* in giving his life as a ransom for all.

Think of his *joy* as the Great Shepherd who carries his lost sheep home to the Father. Notice his *peace* and poise. Watch the *kindness* of his actions to the poor and needy. Trace the sheer *goodness* of his life as he ministers publicly for three years. Meditate on his amazing *faithfulness* both to God and men, even when he felt forsaken by the one and was rejected by the other. Then there is his *gentleness*, to the sick; to the broken hearted; to needy and hopeless sinners. Remember his *self-control* when wicked men mocked and scourged him.

All these qualities are summarised by Luke when he says that the grace of God was on Jesus and he grew in wisdom. In this context wisdom probably means practical spiritual goodness. No wonder God was heard to say that Jesus was his dearly-loved Son, the one with whom he was satisfied!

Sometimes we substitute other things, important in themselves, for real spiritual growth. For example, witnessing to others is a vital part of living the Christian life. But zeal in witness can never substitute for the fruit of the Spirit in our character. Again, knowledge of God's word and an understanding of Christian doctrine plays a vital role in our lives. But when these become a substitute for faithfulness to our friends, gentleness and patience to people we find 'difficult', or are accompanied by a lack of self-control, all our learning and understanding is of little permanent profit. God wants us to grow in grace and in knowledge (2 Pet. 3:18). But even that knowledge is not merely information but personal fellowship with the Lord Jesus Christ!

Some Christians, whether by dint of circumstances or upbringing, or because of the basic tendencies of their personalities are drawn to stress the negative aspects of certain dimensions of the Christian life: self-discipline, rooting out doctrinal error, defending the Christian faith against attack.

These are all biblical duties. But they are not to be pursued in isolation, as some of us tend to do. Someone once humorously remarked to me that it might be possible for a book to be written by some Christians called *You Name it—We're Against it!* Perhaps there was more than a grain of truth in what he said. If we are to let our light shine before men so that, impressed by the character of our lives, they will glorify our Father, we must ask God to send the Holy Spirit to us in order to make us daily more like Jesus.

2. *He grew through the disciplines of life.* A wise Christian once said that spiritual progress should not be measured only by outward evidences. We must also consider the obstacles which were overcome in the process, and the pressures which were endured in order to make such progress.

That is a principle which helps us to think and judge rightly about the actions of others. Some who seem to have made extraordinary headway in the Christian life may have had far fewer and slighter obstacles in their way than others. Some possess qualities by nature which others develop only through arduous spiritual exercise.

Jesus grew in all the positive graces of the Spirit. But the lustre of his character is all the greater because he did so in the face of severe obstacles and constant trials. He once spoke about the whole period of his ministry as a continuous time of trials (Lk. 22:28). As the Captain of our salvation and the Pioneer of the life of faith he experienced opposition from the powers of darkness at the height of their strength. We, by contrast, even though our trials are very real, meet with a foe who has been defeated and stripped of his powers (see Col. 2:15; Heb. 2:14).

What were some of the difficulties faced by our Lord which we also face, and through which we may grow as he grew in grace?

Jesus was tempted. The New Testament goes further: he was tempted in every way, just as we are (Heb. 4:15). Do we have the faith to believe that? When we are tempted we tend to think (although we would be hesitant to admit it): 'Yes, I know he was tempted; but he did not experience what I am experiencing'. *But the truth is the other way round.* You will never experience what he did, because you are a sinner. In our temptations we have given way long before we ever approached the level of temptation's pressure which Jesus experienced. Because we have given in in the past the powers of darkness never need to apply the pressure to us that they applied to Jesus. We provide them with an easy target. Jesus, on the other hand, exhausted all the devil's powers and energies. They could find no 'grip', no 'foothold' in the life of Jesus (Jn. 14:30). According to the Gospel records the powers of darkness mounted an all-out attack on Jesus (a legion of demons was stationed in one man at Gadara in order to ward off Jesus' victory). But even in the hour of the power of darkness they could not overcome him (Lk. 22:53).

Jesus experienced rejection and misunderstanding. One of the most painful things young Christians may experience is the response of their parents to their new found faith.

There are probably many occasions in which we

ourselves, rather than the gospel, cause offence to our parents. Many of us would have to admit that we lose sight of the teaching of God's word, and do not show them the humility, love and obedience which Scripture commands. Sometimes we are far more interested in evangelising them than in obeying them. God's word clearly tells us that the major part of our evangelising our parents (if they are not yet Christians) should be by obedience to them! Perhaps we are too often in a hurry to tell them that we have become Christians. We are not sufficiently patient to allow them to see with their own eyes the changes which begin to take place in our lives. Here again Jesus is a wonderful example. *Do you think he had to tell Mary that the Grace of God was on his life?*

Yet, while we may be at fault as young Christians, there are times when some of Christ's followers will suffer misunderstanding and even persecution at home, and certainly at school, or College, or work. How do we know that Jesus understands? How is he our example then?

Jesus himself grew in grace through the way in which he responded to misunderstanding. This was one of the things which his mother Mary remembered—how she and Joseph had shown misunderstanding of and insensitivity to Jesus. They had taken him with them at the age of twelve to the Temple Services at the Feast of the Passover. What an experience! On their journey home they realised that Jesus was not with their company, returned to Jerusalem and eventually found him in the Temple courts engaged in discussion with the teachers. Mary (how like a mother!) rebuked him: 'Did you not know how worried *your father and I* would be?' Of course they had not even thought of him when they began the journey home! They had probably been engaged with their own group of friends.

Jesus' reply is exquisite. It shows his faithfulness to God and his word, and his desire for Mary and Joseph to discover the real reason for his presence in their family. But Luke records, 'they did not understand what he was saying to them' (Lk. 2:50). It was not the last time there was misunderstanding of Jesus by his family (Mk. 3:21). Nor was it only in this intimate circle that he was to be misunderstood. How often his own disciples seemed to be more like hindrances than helps to his ministry! (See Matt. 8:25–6; 14:25–31; 16:8, 22–3; 17:4–5, 14–20; Lk. 24:25.)

The misunderstanding which Jesus suffered was to lead to his death (1 Cor. 2:8). Yet he did not protest. Rather Jesus kept on showing the fruit of the Spirit. He did not open his mouth in self-defence; he did not raise his voice against those who oppressed him.

> *What grace, O Lord, and beauty shone*
>   *Around Thy steps below!*
> *What patient love was seen in all*
>   *Thy life and death of woe!*
>
> *For ever on Thy burdened heart*
>   *A weight of sorrow hung,*
> *Yet no ungentle, murmuring word*
>   *Escaped Thy silent tongue.*
>
> *Thy foes might hate, despise, revile,*
>   *Thy friends unfaithful prove;*
> *Unwearied in forgiveness still,*
>   *Thy heart could only love.*

The example which Jesus sets before us should encourage us to sing:

> O give us hearts to live like Thee,
> Like Thee, O Lord, to grieve
> Far more for others' sins than all
> The wrongs that we receive.

Edward Denny

3. *He grew in obedience.* Obedience lay at the heart of Jesus' life. The apostles saw his obedience as the key to understanding his whole life and his death on the cross for us. The reason he is able to be the Saviour is because he obeyed God in our place throughout his life and suffered the punishment of our disobedience by his obedience in death.

Part of Jesus' obedience was, of course, unique. It was God's special plan for Jesus alone that he should be asked to lay down his life for others. In this respect also he did the will of his Father (Jn. 4:34; 5:30; 6:38). But Jesus also placed himself under the law of God by which our lives are also governed. He was 'born under law' (Gal. 4:4).

There is an important example of this in the teaching of Luke 2:39–52. What did Jesus do when he discovered that his mother and Joseph were liable to sin? After all, he was the Son of God; he was to die to be their Saviour. Luke tells us (again, undoubtedly on the authority of Mary's testimony) that Jesus 'went down to Nazareth with them *and was obedient to them*' (Lk. 2:51). He honoured his parents. When he was hanging on the cross, in the last agonies of his passion, with his dying breath he made arrangements for the apostle John to care for his mother. Here is obedience to the will of God at its finest. Jesus

responded magnificently to the moral commandments of God's law and exhibited them to perfection in his own life.

4. *He grew through experience*. The Gospels frequently record the response which Jesus made to
different situations. They tell us something of the
wide variety of human experience he had, and the
vast numbers of human needs he encountered.
The impression which we gain is that, as Jesus
increased in experience he seemed to go from
strength to strength in coping with it. Near the
end of his life, when we are told that his own
spirit was deeply troubled and disturbed, he exercised so much grace and self-control that he was
able to encourage his disciples lest their hearts
should also be troubled (Jn. 14:1ff).

The Letter to the Hebrews deals with this aspect of our Lord's experience at some length and
draws out the doctrinal significance of it. He was
God's High Priest. He came to offer a sacrifice,
and at the same time to be the victim himself. But
a High Priest had a further ministry. He prayed for
and cared for God's people. That was why he
needed to come from among them, so that he
could feel for them in their weakness and needs
(Heb. 5:1ff). This is the kind of High Priest and
Saviour we have in Jesus:

> For this reason he had to be made like his
> brothers in every way, in order that he might
> become a merciful and faithful high priest in
> service to God . . . Because he himself suffered
> when he was tempted, he is able to help those
> who are being tempted.
>
> Heb. 2:17–18

For we do not have a high priest who is unable to sympathize with our weaknesses, but we have one who has been tempted in every way, just as we are—yet was without sin.

Heb. 4:15

So, every experience of life was tasted in some form by Jesus. He blazed a Pioneer's trail of total, whole hearted obedience to his Father in every experience. He responded with grace and the fruit of the Spirit in every trial and test. Through everything he grew in stature as a man, and in favour with God and man. Because he is the Captain of our salvation we know that he did all this for our sakes, and as an example to us. Because he is the Pioneer of our faith, we know that he has made it possible for us to follow him. Because he is a High Priest who shares our human nature we know that he is able to help us in our weakness. As our Example, he is also perfectly equipped to be our Guide.

All this raises a further question for us. How did Jesus grow in grace like this? What means did he use? What did he 'feed' his spirit on in order to grow so perfectly? If we can discover the answers to such questions it will be obvious that we must use the same means in order to follow his example and grow more and more like him.

THE MEANS OF JESUS' GROWTH

Jesus did not possess special means of spiritual growth which are not available to us. It is essential to realise this if we are to understand Jesus. It is equally essential to appreciate it if we are to grow like him.

Nowhere did Jesus explicitly tell his disciples what were to be the God-given means by which they would develop as his followers. But when we become familiar with the Gospel narratives it becomes clear that he looked to three particular channels of help and blessing.

Jesus searched the Scriptures. We do so in order to find the meaning of his life and ministry. In fact Jesus did the same thing. It was through his understanding of God's word that he grew in his appreciation of the will of God for his life. Even a single reading of the Gospels makes us realise that Jesus identified himself with the Old Testament figures of the Suffering Servant (Is. 52:13–53:12) and the Son of Man (Dan. 7:9–14). He saw his own life and ministry prophesied in the pages of Scripture, and he lived in order that Scripture might be fulfilled through him.

We too will find out God's will for our lives, and grow in the knowledge of it by searching the Scriptures. There we will find specific directions, principles and examples which will enable us to grow in obedience to God and to increase in our knowledge of him.

Jesus grew in moral obedience by his understanding, use of and obedience to God's word. The classic example of this is in his temptations. There our Lord revealed a rare depth of knowledge and insight into parts of the Book of Deuteronomy. God's word was the Spirit's sword in Jesus' hands, and safeguarded him in a time of fierce temptation.

Such knowledge and understanding of God's word, linked with humble obedience, will always lead to growth in the Christian life.

Jesus found fellowship with God in prayer. His whole life was one of prayer.

Throughout the story of the last three years of his life we are told of the regular periods of prayer Jesus had. They were times of intercession— there was so much for which he had to pray. But they were also times of fellowship and loving communion with his Father. Many students of the Bible have assumed, from the ease with which Judas led the soldiers to the Garden of Gethsemane, that Jesus made a habit of communing with God there whenever he was in Jerusalem. The hills around Galilee were another favourite and much frequented spot.

How did this prayer fellowship help Jesus to grow? *First*, because it was at such times that he enjoyed meditation on his Father's greatness and love. It may have been in such times that the special features of his Father's will were impressed on him. In John 5:20 he says: 'the Father loves the Son and shows him all he does'. This intimate knowledge—like the familiarity which Jesus developed with the skill of Joseph as they worked hour by hour, day by day at the carpenter's bench at Nazareth—was something which developed in times of communion with God. But, *secondly*, in prayer Jesus drew on the resources of God his Father. John's Gospel particularly reveals the depths of relationship between them. But it also appears elsewhere in the Gospels. One of the things for which Jesus prayed was that the Father would glorify his name. It is interesting to notice that Paul says Abraham grew strong in faith *as he gave glory to God* (Rom. 4:20). We can surely assume that, in these hours of prayer, Jesus did exactly the same. As he kept his heart in tune with God and expressed his love and devotion to him, that love and devotion gained in energy and power. That is one of the qualities of love. It grows in the exercise.

Jesus looked for fellowship with God's people. Was that not what he was doing at the age of twelve in the Temple? He was engaged in discussion with the teachers. He was asking penetrating questions which amazed these theologians. He was wrestling with the great issues which God's word had already begun to impress on his spirit. Did he know something of what Luke was later to describe as 'the burning heart' (Lk. 24:32) as he discussed the Old Testament's teaching with these learned men? Was he inwardly grateful to his Father that, for all their faults, here were men who delighted to discuss the ways of God with his people. Did Jesus, as a boy look on these leaders of his people, as he was later to look on a young ruler, and love them?

At the age of thirty he chose twelve disciples. He wanted to send them out. Eventually he planned to send them into the entire known world to preach the gospel to every creature! But he had also chosen them 'to be with him' (Mk. 3:14). Of course they needed to be with him for their own sake. But did he not want and need companionship for his own sake, in order to grow in fellowship with them? Did he not take three of them with him to share in the holy experience when he was changed on the Mount of Transfiguration (Mk. 9:2–13), and to witness his sufferings and encourage him by his presence with him in Gethsemane (Mk. 14:33–42)? Why did he go to Bethany, to the home of Mary, Martha and Lazarus? It was undoubtedly because he found in their spiritual fellowship and love an atmosphere which helped him in his spiritual pilgrimage.

Knowledge of God's word; communion in God's presence; fellowship with God's people. These are the means by which Jesus grew in grace.

Have we begun to use these same means? We shall need to return to them again in the course of the following chapters. But for the moment we ought to remind ourselves that they are matters of priority. If we are to grow; if we are to become increasingly like Christ, then we will need to follow the Master's example.

If you have not already begun to do that, begin today. Indeed, begin now.

SECTION TWO
BASIC PRINCIPLES

What are the essential marks of spiritual growth? How are they produced in our lives by God?

In this section three of these marks are considered. The Christian grows in the knowledge of God. What does that mean? Secondly, he develops a desire to know God, and to live more closely to him. What produces this desire? Thirdly, he must come to a deeper understanding of his Saviour and what he has done for him. He must be willing to make the sacrifices involved in being a Christian. What does that involve?

3: In The Beginning

In chapter one we saw that Jesus grew, not only physically but also in spiritual stature and power. In particular we are told that he grew *in wisdom* (Lk. 2:52).

If we now ask: 'What does Luke mean when he says that Jesus grew in wisdom?' we must turn back to the rest of the Bible to discover the answer. It tells us something which sounds strange, almost unwelcome to our modern ears: *The beginning of wisdom is the fear of the Lord* (Prov. 1:7; 9:10). To say that Jesus grew in wisdom is simply another way of saying that he lived in the fear of God.

A Jesus who *feared* God sounds an unfamiliar Jesus to us. A Jesus who trusted God, who loved God—yes! But do we not hesitate to say or even to think that Jesus *feared* God? We are tempted to say: 'Well, I have never heard this before. No sermon or Bible study I ever heard described Jesus as a God-fearer. And, quite frankly, I am not sure that this is the Jesus I know and follow. Is this the Bible's Jesus?'

Yet the equation seems undeniable. Jesus grew in wisdom. Wisdom means learning to fear God. If Jesus grew in wisdom he must have grown also in the fear of God.

The problem is that we often have a rather one-sided view of Jesus. But we also tend to have a very distorted view of the Bible's teaching on the fear of God. One wise old writer once wrote that the fear of God 'is generally looked upon as a left-handed grace': He meant that because it is there in the Bible we have to recognise it. Yet we feel ill-at-ease about the whole idea that there should be fear of any kind in spiritual life.

We shall never understand this dimension of growth in grace—either in Christ's life or in our own—until we realise that the Bible speaks about two very different kinds of fear.

TWO KINDS OF FEAR

The Bible speaks about what is called 'servile fear' and also about 'filial fear'. These technical expressions simply mean the kind of fear which a slave would feel towards a harsh and unyielding master, and the kind of loving fear which a child feels towards his father. Servile fear is the kind of fear which people often know before they become Christians. It is a sense of terror of God. Filial fear should be the experience of every true child of God. *The mistake we often make in thinking about fear is to imagine that all fear is servile fear.* If we can avoid that mistake, discover the meaning of filial fear and grow in the experience of it new strength will inevitably come into our Christian living.

What is servile fear? Thomas Manton, at one time a chaplain to Oliver Cromwell, described it like this:

> *Servile*, by which a man feareth God and hateth him, as a slave feareth a cruel master, whom he could wish dead, and himself rid of his service, and obeyeth by mere compulsion and constraint. Thus the wicked fear God because they

have drawn an ill picture of him in their minds: Matt. 25:24,5, 'I knew thou wast a hard man, and I was afraid'. They perform only a little unwilling and unpleasing service, and as little as they can, because of their ill conceit (mistaken and perverted understanding) of God.

For all the old-fashioned language in Manton's statement there is a good deal in what he says. It rings true to modern experience. If we think of the fear of God only in this way it is not surprising that we find it difficult to believe that it is the beginning of wisdom, or that Jesus knew anything about it.

But often the deepest reason for our distaste and dislike of the idea of the fear of God is that this kind of servile fear lurks within our own hearts even after we have become Christians. Sometimes it may haunt a true Christian throughout the whole of his spiritual life. He may spend years trying to hide from the fact that hidden within our own lives lurks a spirit of servile fear which we have never properly faced and from which we have never been fully delivered! What we must learn is that the only means of deliverance lies in our growth in filial fear. It takes filial fear to destroy servile fear!

What then is filial fear? It is that indefinable mixture of reverence, fear, pleasure, joy and awe which fills our hearts when we realise who God is and what he has done for us. It is a love for God which is so great that we would be ashamed to do anything which would displease or grieve him, and makes us happiest when we are doing his will. Perhaps it has never been better expressed, with its mysterious combination of pleasure and awe, than in F. W. Faber's words:

My fear of Thee, O Lord, exults
  Like life within my veins,
A fear which rightly claims to be
One of love's sacred pains.

There is no joy the soul can meet
  Upon life's various road
Like the sweet fear that sits and shrinks
  Under the eye of God.

Oh Thou art greatly to be feared,
  Thou art so prompt to bless!
The dread to miss such love as Thine
  Makes fear but love's excess.

But fear is love, and love is fear,
  And in and out they move;
But fear is an intenser joy
  Than mere unfrightened love.

They love Thee little, if at all,
  Who do not fear Thee much;
If love is Thine attraction, Lord!
  Fear is Thy very touch.

How little we know of these biblical paradoxes!
Psalm 2 encourages us to 'Serve the Lord with fear
and rejoice with trembling'. Psalm 112 tells us of
the blessing experienced by the man who fears
the Lord. It is against this kind of background that
we begin to understand that when Jesus grew
in wisdom one of the experiences which accompanied his growth was the sense of joy and
awe he discovered in the presence of his heavenly
Father.

THE FEAR OF THE LORD

We are commanded to fear God (1 Pet. 2:17 cf. 1:17). We are expected to fear Christ (Eph. 5:21). Many other New Testament passages teach us that the fear of the Lord is not simply to be dismissed as 'Old Testament religion'. It is the heart and soul of New Testament Christianity as well. Ever since God called a people to himself his desire has been that they should live in a relationship with him of filial fear.

When the Ten Commandments are repeated in Moses' great exhortation to God's people in the Book of Deuteronomy, the people are reminded of God's heart-longings for them: 'Oh, that their hearts would be inclined to fear me and keep all my commands always, so that it might go well with them and their children for ever!' (Deut. 5:29)

Later in the Old Testament prophets like Jeremiah were beginning to look forward to the new covenant which God would make through Christ. God promised to accomplish what he himself longed to see in the lives of his people: 'I will give them singleness of heart and action, so that they will always fear me for their own good and the good of their children after them. I will make an everlasting covenant with them: I will never stop doing good to them, and I will inspire them to fear me, so that they will never turn away from me' (Jer. 32:39–40).

These words contain God's answer to the prayer of David: 'Give me an undivided heart, *that I may fear your name*' (Ps. 86:11). God looks for filial fear in his children; they pray for it; he provides it by the inward ministry of his Holy Spirit!

But David's prayer also suggests that a failure to

fear God in this special way is the result of a divided heart, one that is not entirely devoted to God and does not submit to him with whole-hearted abandon. Our Lord Jesus devoted all his powers to God; he had an undivided heart. That is why his life is the supreme illustration of what it means to fear the Lord. It is the beginning of wisdom, or practical holiness, because it is born in an undivided heart, a pure heart. Such a heart, Jesus said, 'sees God' (Matt. 5:8). It therefore fears God (because it has seen him as he is). But it also learns to see life and to live it on the basis of such intimate knowledge of God. It is this which makes the life of the God-fearing child of a heavenly Father so different.

We must try to think a little more about the source of this fear of God and then about the transformation which it produces in our Christian lives.

THE SOURCE OF FILIAL FEAR

In some passages in Scripture the expression 'the fear of God' is simply another way of speaking about the presence of God, or God making his presence known (e.g. Gen. 20:11; Ex. 20:20). God himself is the ultimate source of filial fear. It is his presence which produces that answering response in our hearts. We catch a sense of his greatness and majesty, and a silence comes over us (cf. Job 40:3-5; 42:2-6).

But we have not yet touched the nerve centre of the fear of God when we have said this. For the child of God there is a deeper mystery to be unfolded. He can say with John Newton "Twas grace that taught my heart to fear', and with the writer of Psalm 130: 'There is forgiveness with you, that you may be feared'.

What does this mean? It means that filial fear, the fear of a son for his Father, is produced by God's love for us. More exactly, it is the result of discovering that the God whom we thought of with slavish, servile fear, the holy righteous, terrifying God of judgment and majesty, is also the God who forgives us through Jesus Christ. He is just, yet he justifies the ungodly. He is righteous, yet he counts sinners as righteous. One of the reasons why we know so little of such filial fear today is that we do not appreciate the glory of the gospel! If we would grow in grace so that we fear God like this, we must first return to the fundamental truths of the gospel, and to the meaning of the cross.

The great illustration of this, as we shall later see in greater detail, is Simon Peter. When he discovered how weak and sinful he had proved to be in denying his Master, he looked round only to discover his Master's eyes gazing upon him from the other side of the courtyard. What a moment! 'The Lord turned and looked at Peter. And Peter remembered what the Lord had said . . . and Peter went out and wept bitterly' (Lk. 22:61–2).

Was Peter ashamed? Of course he was. But he also wept because of what he had seen in the eyes of Christ. They said to him: 'Remember what I said Peter—that you would deny me, but that I would pray for you (Lk. 22:31–2). I am praying for you, Peter, because I still love you. I forgive you. I am going out tomorrow to die on the cross for you.' Do you not think that Peter's heart responded in words very like these?

O how I fear Thee, living God,
With deepest tenderest fears,

43

And worship Thee with trembling hope
And penitential tears.

Filial fear is always the grateful response of
sinners who have become saints.

Why then is it important to grow in the fear of
God? Because the effects which this produces are
themselves marks of spiritual growth.

THE EFFECTS OF FILIAL FEAR

(i) The first effect of the fear of the Lord is that it
tends to take away all other fears. Jesus said it is by
learning to fear God that we are delivered from the
fear of what men will do to us (Mt. 10:26). He
illustrated the power of such filial fear in his own
life. Because he would die rather than grieve his
Father's heart he was not bullied by the threats of
what others might do to him. Because we are
working through the implications of our salvation in the fear of God (Phil. 2:12) we do not
need to be frightened in any way by those who
oppose us, says Paul (Phil. 1:28). Even if we
suffer, says Peter (who surely knew what he was
talking about), we do not need to fear what those
who do us harm fear (1 Pet. 3:13–14).

It was said of John Knox, the boldest of all
Scottish Christians, that he feared the face of no
man (or woman, as Mary Queen of Scots was to
discover, although she towered above him by
some six inches!). The reason was that he had
learned to fear the face of God. This is the secret of
Christian courage and boldness.

(ii) The second effect of fearing God is that we are
kept by it from continuing in sin. There are many
examples of this in the Bible.

When Moses was given the Ten Commandments the people were awed by the sense of the
majesty of God they experienced at Mount Sinai.
Moses explained why God had touched their
hearts in this way: 'Do not be afraid. God has come
to test you, so that *the fear of God will be with you
to keep you from sinning*' (Ex. 20:20). That was
exactly the spirit which had kept Moses himself
alive as a child. When Pharaoh had ordered every
new born boy to be slaughtered, we are told, 'The
midwives, however, *feared God and did not do
what the king of Egypt had told them to do*; they let
the boys live' (Ex. 1:17). Rather than destroy the
God-given privileges of life, these ladies refused
to obey the king. They feared God; they would do
nothing to grieve him, no matter what it cost
them.

(iii) This filial fear of God puts *integrity* into
Christian character. The child of God who pos-
sesses it is straightforward. His word is his bond.
He does not engage in double-dealing, for he
'makes holiness complete, in the fear of God, and
cleanses himself from every defilement of body
and spirit' (2 Cor. 7:1).

Nehemiah was such a man. He was brought up
in a harsh tradition of governing the people in his
charge. But he did not follow the precedent which
had been set before him, for one reason, as he
explained: 'The former governors who were
before me laid heavy burdens upon the people . . .
Even their servants lorded it over the people. But I
do not do so, *because of the fear of God*' (Neh.
5:15). Fearing God enables the Christian to say
'No' when that becomes necessary. And for some
of us, saying 'No' is one of the last lessons we
seem to be able to learn.

(iv) The other side of this integrity is that filial

fear promotes obedience in our lives. We not only avoid doing what is wrong, but we very much want to do what is right and pleasing in the sight of God.

Noah provides us with an interesting example of this. By faith, he built an ark 'in holy fear' (Heb. 11:7). Because he so highly valued the smile of God on his life he was unafraid of the undoubted leg-pulling (and worse) which he experienced. After all, he was building an ark on dry land, in readiness for the Day of Judgment. But God had spoken to him; Noah would rather lose all his 'friends' than lose the friendship of God. He knew something of the experience about which Charles Wesley wrote:

> O give me, Lord, the tender heart
> That trembles at the approach of sin;
> A godly fear of sin impart,
> Implant and root it deep within,
> That I may dread Thy gracious power
> And never dare offend Thee more.

(v) But there is a further, and perhaps unexpected consequence of such filial fear. *The fear of God produces effectiveness in evangelism*. At least there can be no doubting that this was the case in the life-style of the first Christian churches.

Take their services of worship as an example. What did Paul look for in them? He expected that there would be such a sense of the presence of God with his people that outsiders (non-Christians) coming in would be immediately arrested by it. Such a person would sense that God was present in holiness and power; the secrets of their own hearts would be revealed. He would fall on his face and say: 'Surely God is here among you all' (1 Cor. 14:24–5) Why did Paul expect this? Because he knew that this was often the result of Christians walking in the fear of the Lord. In the days surrounding his own conversion 'the church . . . had peace and was built up; and walking in the fear of the Lord and in the comfort of the Holy Spirit it was multiplied' (Acts 9:31). Later on in Acts we read of another situation when 'fear fell upon them all; and the name of the Lord Jesus was extolled' (Acts 19:17). It needs to be emphasised again and again that this was not servile fear, but filial fear. It was joyful fear, penitential joy, trembling hope. But it put something into the living and worshipping of those early Christians which we need to recover in our own lives.

The same is true at an individual as well as a corporate level. Paul could say that it was because he had experienced the 'fear of the Lord' that he wanted to persuade men to trust in Christ (2 Cor. 5:11). This is one of the most revealing statements he ever made about his inner thoughts on the theme of evangelism. He holds this statement together with another which may even appear contradictory: 'the love of Christ constrains us' (2 Cor. 5:14). But the two belong very naturally together. For it was at the judgment seat of Christ that Paul had learned there was forgiveness with Christ in order that he might be feared (Ps. 130:4). He had been taken there by the Holy Spirit and convinced of his sin, of his lack of righteousness and of the certainty of judgment to come (Jn. 16:8–11). But he found there mercy and forgiveness. When a man has seen that, and been there, he no longer thinks that the fear of the Lord and the love of the Lord are mutually exclusive. He discovers that one cannot exist without the

presence of the other. He then begins to understand with Paul that evangelism is not merely a
privilege; it is a debt. We owe the gospel to our
fellow men. We offend God our Father if we do
not take it to them (Rom. 1:14). We who have
learned to fear him will not dare to offend him.

GROWING IN THE FEAR OF GOD

How then are we to grow in this essential
Christian grace? Scripture sets before us many
great thoughts about God which will lead us, as
they led Jesus, to a loving filial reverence and fear
of our Father in heaven.

Consider first that God has chosen you. Yes,
you did choose to serve him; but only because he
first loved and chose you. The very mystery of the
relationship between God's choice of us and our
choice of God should lead us to fear him.

Then there is God's providence. Every hair of
my head is numbered! He has guided me, protected me, chastised me, provided for my needs
from the day I was born. More, he has over-ruled
the circumstances in which I was born. The very
genes from which I come were not beyond his
sovereign rule.

Think then about his saving grace. The gift of
his Son; the sending of his Spirit to claim me
personally as his child; the way in which he
moulds my life in his service. Think too on a
larger canvas. For salvation is of the Jews (Jn.
4:22). Its coming to the Gentiles (to our Western
world) was the result of its rejection by the Jews.
We, says Paul, are really wild branches un-
naturally grafted in. Do not therefore be high-
minded, he concludes, 'but fear' (Rom. 11:20).

These are all thoughts which are calculated to produce this filial fear of God in our hearts. Fearing God is the fruit of the gospel; it is the beginning of real practical wisdom. That is why Ecclesiastes (that shrewd preacher in the Old Testament whose sharp pen exposes so many contemporary fallacies) tells us:

> Here is the conclusion of the matter
> Fear God and keep his commandments,
>   for this is the whole duty of man.
>
> Ecclesiastes 12:13

If we have never grown beyond servile fear, either in our experience or our understanding these will seem dismal and depressing words in the extreme.

But if we know the filial, loving fear of God as our Father, we will realise that this is not only our whole duty, it is also the beginning of true spiritual progress. So wrote John Flavel, a man of great spiritual insight from a former generation:

> The carnal person fears man, not God;
>   the strong Christian fears God, not man;
>   the weak Christian fears man too much,
>   and God too little.

How true!

4: A Spiritual Appetite

The Book of Psalms has been described as 'an anatomy of all the parts of the soul'. It is an excellent description. For what we find in the Psalms is a description and analysis of the spiritual life. Nothing is hidden from us. 'Highs' and 'lows' are alike recorded. That is why, when we turn to read the Psalms we are often amazed by the way they seem to present a mirror-image of our own experiences and condition.

Sometimes in the Psalms we see a description of our own experience. But sometimes we also recognise a description of new experiences. These provide insights and guidelines for us, to teach us what to anticipate. Some Psalms are really saying to us: 'This is how God may work. Be prepared to recognise his hand in your life in similar experiences'.

In this chapter we shall look at the experience which is described in two consecutive Psalms—42 and 43. They are unusually appropriate at this juncture of our thinking about spiritual growth.

These two Psalms belong together. Psalm 43 is one of only two Psalms in the second book of the Psalter (Pss. 42–72) which has no title. The reason almost certainly is that at one time it was joined with Psalm 42. The theme of both Psalms is the same. Indeed you will probably have noticed that there is a chorus or refrain running through both of them (Ps. 42:5,11; 43:5):

> *Why are you downcast, O my soul?*
> *Why so disturbed within me?*
> *Put your hope in God,*
> *for I will yet praise him,*
> *my Saviour and my God.*

No wonder the message of these Psalms has often been taken to be 'counsel for the spiritually depressed'. They certainly provide such counsel. But that is probably not meant to be the main lesson. For it is characteristic of the Psalms to introduce the chief theme, not in the chorus, but in the opening words. Psalm 42 begins with this statement:

> *As the deer pants for streams of water*
> *so my soul pants for you, O God.*
> *My soul thirsts for God, for the living God.*
> *When can I go and meet with God?*

Here is someone who is longing to know God! That is an essential part of all true spiritual growth. Of course growing as a Christian involves gaining more knowledge of God's word; it implies a life of prayer and witness. But these are all the results of something much more basic. Being a Christian means knowing God. Growing as a Christian means increasing in our desire to know God. This is the sum of the Christian life. Jesus himself said: 'This is eternal life: *that they may know you*, the only true God' (Jn. 17:3). The true men and women of faith are 'the people who know their God' (Dan. 11:32). That is why, in the Old Testament, one of the anticipated blessings of the new age which the Messiah would inaugurate was that then men and women would 'know the Lord' (Jer. 31:34). This is the very heart of the Christian life. It is fundamental to all spiritual growth. If we are not growing in the knowledge of God, we are not growing at all.

Does it sound churlish to suggest that our greatest weakness today as Christians (young and old) lies here? That was the complaint of Hosea against his contemporary church. God's people were destroyed for lack of knowledge (Hos. 4:6). Similarly we tend to be a generation of Christians who major on minor matters but do not seem to possess the true treasure of the gospel in the knowledge of God. We do not really know God. At best we know about him.

The man who wrote Psalms 42 and 43 may once have been content with a similar level of spiritual experience. But then God himself began to order his circumstances in such a way that a new desire to grow spiritually filled his horizon. He began to long to know God. He describes his experience in three stages.

A DESCRIPTION OF HIS LONGING TO KNOW GOD

What is it like to have a desire to know God? The first thing that is clear from these Psalms is that it can be an exceedingly painful and disturbing thing. This man felt he was cast down. He began by realising that he did not know God as he needed to:

> Why are you downcast, O my soul?
> Why so disturbed within me?

Perhaps in his earlier days he had known the presence of God in powerful ways. But now his spirit felt barren and dry. It was parched, and he was crying out for the dew of God's presence to come to revive and restore him.

It is a great temptation, looking at this man's condition, to say that he was simply a defeated and disobedient child of God—a backslider. But one of the very interesting things about what he says is the fact that he makes no mention of repentance, or of any specific sin which is barring him from the presence of God. This is not one of the *Psalms of Penitence*. Indeed, in some ways the reverse is true. For here is a man who can address God as 'my Rock' (v.9). He is thinking of God as his shelter and protection—as a Crag in which he can hide to find shelter and protection from his enemies. 'At night' he confesses, 'his song is with me' (v.8). Hardly the words of a backslider!

The truth of the matter is that God has begun to break up the fallow ground in his spirit (Jer. 4:3; Hos. 10:12). He plans to bring him on to a new stage of spiritual experience. As in ordinary life, so in spiritual life, we experience not only the traumas of birth, but the pangs of growing out of one stage into another stage of life.

But what were the means God employed in his life to bring about this new state of affairs? And, correspondingly, what pattern of experiences may we anticipate he will employ in our lives to bring us into a growing knowledge of him and his ways with us?

THE CAUSES OF HIS NEW SPIRITUAL DESIRES

There are three things which God began to use:

1. *Memories of the past*. As he called to God in his perplexity, he said 'These things I remember as I pour out my soul'. In his mind's eye he was back

in Jerusalem. He saw the crowds of pilgrims at one of the great festival services of the Religious Year: 'I used to go with the multitude'. He remembered the atmosphere: 'shouts of joy and thanksgiving'. He himself was at the head of the procession (v.4). It all comes flooding back to him—he even uses a rare word in the original which conveys the picture of the short, careful steps it is always necessary to take in a vast crowd to avoid everyone running into one another.

Yes, those were wonderful days! Sometimes looking back like that can be a symptom of spiritual decay. If all our hopes, all our finest experiences lie in the past and all we do is to complain that things are no longer what they once were, it usually is a sign of personal spiritual decay. But that was not the case with this man. He was remembering the grace and power of God's presence with his people for a specific reason: *to stir up his soul to long for and anticipate it again.* That is one of the things a memory is for!

When Paul was concerned about the spiritual growth of his young friend and lieutenant Timothy, he encouraged him to use his memory. Remember the day we laid our hands on you, Paul said: Think of that occasion when the Holy Spirit set you apart through us. Do you not recall how God sealed your calling and wonderfully blessed us? Do you not remember how you gave yourself to the Lord out of an abundant sense of his goodness to you? Remember that hour, Timothy, and let its memory stir you up to seek and to serve God now (see 2 Tim. 1:6–7; 1 Tim. 4:14).

Many of us have similar memories of times of unusual blessing in our lives. George Whitefield the great 18th century evangelist used to say that when he returned to Oxford University (where he had studied) he always had a strong desire to go to the spot where he had been converted and kiss the ground. The memory of what God had done for him, and how he had met with him had proved to be such a great source of continuing blessing that this was the only way he felt he could express his gratitude!

I remember meeting a very elderly Christian in the far north of Scotland. For many years there had been little or no faithful preaching of Christ in the area where he had his little croft. I wondered how he had managed to keep his spiritual fervour (Rom. 12:11). He told me of an event in his teens which had made such an impression on him that he had found enormous encouragement for many many years simply by remembering it. At that time the Lord's supper was celebrated only twice each year. The congregation gathered for several days of special services. On the Sunday afternoon, he had gone out to the back of his father's croft, and was astonished to discover the ground covered in black. Scarcely a blade of grass was to be seen. 'It was' he explained 'because the men all wore black suits, and they were kneeling and bowing together in prayer outside the house, calling on God for "the divine unction"'. There had been such a sense of the Lord's presence that he had never forgotten the occasion. Since then he had continued to long to know the Lord more and more.

Do you have a memory of meeting with God like this? Is it as clear in your mind as the memories which the Psalmist was recalling? Then let your memory accomplish what God means it to: let it create in you a thirst, a longing, a fresh desire to know God and to sense his presence with you the way you did then.

2. *Isolation in the present.* Why was it that all these things were just memories? He tells us: 'I will remember you from the land of Jordan, the heights of Hermon—from Mount Mizar'. The reason he has only recollections is that he is now far away from the scenes of his former blessing. He is miles from Jerusalem, isolated in the highlands. He is cut off from the thriving fellowship of God's people he once knew; he no longer is able to benefit from the various ministries he had formerly enjoyed. There were few resources *here* to encourage his spiritual growth; few friends with whom to share fellowship with God.

The problem was magnified by another factor. There, in Jerusalem, he had been more than simply one among many. He had been a leader, perhaps *the* leader: 'These things I remember . . . how I used to go with the multitude, *leading* the procession to the house of God (Ps. 42:4).

He was not the last to go through such an acute sense of isolation. How many missionaries experience this! At home they played key roles in their own Christian fellowships. They were leaders. But, removed across the face of the earth, far from being leaders they cannot even speak the language of the people. For many months they may feel they are less than members, never mind leaders! When they return home they may experience exactly the same in reverse. While they have been labouring overseas their contemporaries have moved on in life another four years or more. Returning missionaries do not 'fit in' quite so easily as before. Even their own church is at a different stage of development, of which they may no longer feel an integral part.

But we do not need to go overseas to experience

isolation. Any 'life event' can bring the same symptoms. Any major readjustment in our life-style can have this effect of making us feel distanced, disorientated, no longer fulfilling a strategic, purposeful role in our Christian lives. A change of job, of house, of neighbourhood can do this. Bereavement, children leaving home, retirement can do the same.

What did God want to teach the Psalmist? What does he want to teach us in similar situations? *God wants to teach us lessons in isolation which he cannot teach us, or which we cannot learn, in fellowship.* In our loneliness and separation from God's people we may learn to look to God, trust in God, desire God's presence. We discover that in the past we have relied too much on the encouragement of others and insufficiently on the Lord himself. While before we knew God (quite legitimately) through the help of our fellow Christians, now we must learn to know him for ourselves.

This is why the Psalm is called a *Maskil*, that is a song of instruction. The writer is saying to us: This is what God taught me through my experience; it is what he may want to teach you too.

3. *A hostile environment.* He is like a deer roving over the crags and rocks in the height of summer looking for water with which to slake his thirst. But he feels more than thirsty; he feels pursued:

> *As pants the hart for cooling streams*
> *When heated in the chase*
> *So longs my soul O God for thee*
> *And thy refreshing grace.*

There are several indications of this in what he says. Men say to him 'Where is your God?' (v.3).

He goes about mourning 'oppressed by the enemy' (v.9). He prays to be rescued 'from deceitful and wicked men' (Ps. 43:1). No wonder he felt that God had cast him off (Ps. 43:2) . . . He must have felt as though God were digging his spiritual grave. He could not stand the pressure much longer. 'Vindicate me, O God, and plead my cause' he cried (Ps. 43:1).

What was happening to him? There are several strands to be untangled in his experience. God was showing him how much he needed to depend on him for protection. Perhaps at an earlier stage in his experience he felt that he could hold his own with anyone who opposed his faith. Now he was discovering how vulnerable he was. Perhaps too he had taken an altogether too confident view of his own ability to stand firm against the forces of darkness. Now he was beginning to realise that belonging to the kingdom of God meant being a target for the attacks of the Devil. He goes around like a roaring lion, seeking someone to devour. He had sent his emissaries to devour this man in no uncertain terms. He needed help!

Yet none of this lay outside the control of God himself. While the psalmist felt that God was digging his grave he was only partly right. In a sense he was. For he was wanting the man to come to an end of himself and his self confidence. That is always the place where the true knowledge of God begins. But it was not really a grave God was digging at all. It was a well! For out of the depths of this experience would flow a river of spiritual blessing for him, and through him to others. Through it all he was coming to know God. No price was too great to pay for that.

Sometimes we sing:

> *I thirst, I sigh, I faint to prove*
> *The greatness of redeeming love*
> *The love of Christ to me.*

What we tend to learn all too slowly is that sometimes we do have to *thirst*, *sigh* and *faint* if we are
to prove it.

This writer did prove it. So he shares with us
one final thing:

THE SATISFYING OF HIS DESIRES

His testimony is this. He prayed for spiritual
satisfaction. In particular he focused his prayers
on the twin means by which God would bring this
into his life:

> Send forth your light and your truth,
>   let them guide me;
> let them bring me to your holy mountain,
>   to the place where you dwell.
> Then will I go to the altar of God,
>   to God, my joy and my delight.
> I will praise you with the harp,
>   O God, my God.

(Ps. 43:3–4)

What were the means he expected God to use in
order to bring him to a deeper knowledge of him?
How does God meet our desire to know him
better?

1. *The word of God.* When he prays for God's light
and truth he can mean only one thing. It is God's
word which serves as a lamp to our feet and a light
for our path (Ps. 119:105). So another writer confesses:

The entrance of your words gives light;
 it gives understanding to the simple.
I open my mouth and pant,
 longing for your commands.

(Ps. 119:130–1)

What does he mean? Of course he is missing the opportunity to read God's word with others. He has no access to the exposition of God's word in public. But he is wanting much more than the restoration of these lost opportunities. He is asking for God to '*send forth*' his light and truth. He is looking for 'the *entrance* of your words'. This is something quite special.

When we become Christians we are brought out of darkness into God's marvellous light (1 Pet. 2:9). God, whose creation began when he said 'Let light shine out of darkness' has shined in our hearts to bring us to know him through Christ (2 Cor. 4:6). Formerly we were darkness, but now we are light in the Lord (Eph. 5:8). One of the things which accompanies this is the penetration of God's truth into our minds, consciences and hearts. We see our lives in his light for the first time. We are brought to see the kingdom of God for the first time (Jn. 3:3), and we are given a radically new interpretation of our own lives. Illumination, enlightenment seems to take place (cf. Heb. 6:4). It is very common for young Christians to experience this effect of God's word very regularly. There is so much that is new to learn. I have never forgotten the first occasion on which I heard someone preach on the idea that every Christian is a 'saint' according to the New Testament; nor the first time that I appreciated that I was 'in Christ'. These new truths about our lives as Christians often come to us with unforgettable force.

Accompanying this illumination of the mind there is a deliverance and cleansing in our lives. Chains which formerly bound us fast, habits which we could not break seem to be overwhelmed and defeated by God's power. We are not yet perfect (far from it); but we have certainly begun to taste the powers of the age to come (Heb. 6:5). We are new creatures:

> At times with sudden glory,
> He speaks, and all is done;
> Without one stroke of battle
> The victory is won,
> While we, with joy beholding,
> Can scarce believe it true
> The even our kingly Jesus
> Can form such hearts anew.
>
> Charitie Lees de Chenez

But it is not only in the lives of recent converts that God is able to do this. He can speak with unusual power whenever he pleases. He can bring fresh illumination, delivering grace, strong assurance. The psalmist was praying for nothing less than this in his own life. There are times in our experience when ordinary means of growth need to be accompanied by special illumination from God if we are ever to make any significant progress. It was such a time in this man's life. It may also be in our lives too.

2. *The worship of God.* Having prayed for God to come to him, he vows that in response he will come to God. He will climb God's 'holy mountain' (v.3); he will go to the altar of God; he will

find God as 'my joy and my delight' (v.4).

He has now discovered, as we shall discover, that all the experiences of life are ordered by the Lord for one great purpose. Trials and difficulties especially have this purpose in view. It is that our lives should be brought into the presence of God, so that we worship him with all our hearts. This is an authentic sign of spiritual growth.

There is a special significance in the *order* of these words: he climbs the hill; he goes to the altar; he discovers God as his great joy. He is thinking of coming to Jerusalem, where God has promised to reveal himself in his Temple. He is thinking of drawing near to God at the place where sacrifice is made. He believes that on the other side of the altar, because of the sacrifice, he will meet with God in grace and in power.

The order of spiritual experience has not changed since the psalmist's day. It remains the same for us. We need to go to the place where God has promised to meet with us. That is no longer in Jerusalem. It is in Christ. No longer in a place, but now in a person. We too need to climb the hill to God—the hill of Calvary, in order to come to him in whom alone God makes his presence known to us.

What do we find there? We too find an altar cross; a place of sacrifice. We find a victim, our Lord Jesus Christ. We are called to present our bodies on the altar as offerings of thankfulness for his sacrifice for us. This is our spiritual worship (see Rom. 12:1–2). Only on the other side of it shall we discover God as our chief joy.

God has made us to '*glorify* and *enjoy* him for ever'. Are we afraid of the cost of glorifying him? Have we never experienced the bliss of enjoying him here and now. There needs to be a new willingness to sacrifice our lives to him and for him, in order that we may know him fully.

We came upon the writer of Psalms 42 and 43 picturing himself as a thirsty seeker. He longed to know God. We leave him as one who has begun to discover the blessings of a promise which he never heard, but which is so familiar to us. Since we have 'better promises' (Heb. 8:6), let us follow on to know the Lord (Heb. 6:3):

> Jesus said: If a man is thirsty, let him come to me and drink. Whoever believes in me, as the Scripture has said, streams of living water will flow from within him.
>
> (Jn. 7:37)

and again he said: Whoever drinks the water I give him will never thirst. Indeed, the water I give him will become in him a spring of water welling up to eternal life.

> (Jn. 4:14)

The first step forward in knowing God better is the awareness that you do not yet know him fully. It is 'thirsting' for God. It is discovering that he has water which can satisfy our deepest longings. It is saying to him: 'Lord, give me this water' (Jn. 4:15).

Do you *really* know God? Do you realise *how little* you know him? Do you *want* to grow? Are you *willing* for all that is involved? We shall see in the next chapter just exactly what is involved in knowing God better.

5: A Matter of Life and Death

The apostle Paul's relationships with the many congregations in his care were, on the whole, happy and fruitful. But there were some exceptions.

The congregation in Galatia became a burden to him. So did the church at Corinth, and also the fellowship at Colosse. In each case false teachers and false teaching were among the reasons for Paul's concern. When he wrote to these churches he was always concerned to provide therapy for their spiritual ailments. In particular he was concerned about how, in these different congregations a similar pattern had begun to emerge. In one way or another they were being tempted to look for something *extra*, to find a 'plus' in their Christian experience which would bring them up to a new level of spiritual growth. The 'plus' was different in each case. But in every case it involved the teaching that Christ himself was not enough. If people were really to know God, it was suggested, then they would need to have something extra.

The trouble was that instead of growing in grace these Christians were 'falling from grace' (Gal. 5:4). They had begun to lose sight of what the grace of God really is and does. It was therefore vital that Paul should recall them to appreciate and enjoy the grace of God offered to them in the Lord Jesus Christ.

It is a fixed principle that spiritual growth will

always involve understanding, appreciating, receiving and enjoying the grace of God. So Paul found it in his own experience. 'I am what I am' he wrote, *by the grace of God* (1 Cor. 15:10). Grace is so absolutely vital for spiritual development that we usually speak about it in terms of the biblical expression which provides the title for this book: growing *in grace*. But what is growing *in grace*? What is grace? What is involved in receiving it? How does it come to us, and what are its implications for us?

It is interesting to notice that when Paul wrote to these three churches who caused him so much heartache he had one common message. The Corinthians were searching for their 'plus' by grossly over-emphasising the gifts of the Spirit to the point of ignoring the fruit of the Spirit. The Galatians were emphasising the necessity of the rite of circumcision as an 'extra' to the point of dis-gracing God's free grace. The Colossians were adding rules and regulations to the Christian life and leading those who had begun their Christian lives through faith to walk by legalistic principles.

What was Paul's common message in this situation? What message could lead these difficult congregations away from their errors, rescue them from their immaturity and help them to progress in the grace of God? Paul's answer was to emphasise the meaning and message of the cross. *To the Colossians* he wrote:

When you were dead in your sins and in the uncircumcision of your sinful nature, God made you alive with Christ. He forgave us all our sins, having canceled the written code, with its regulations, that was against us and that stood opposed to us; he took it away, nailing it to the cross. And having disarmed the powers and authorities, he made a public spectacle of them, triumphing over them by the cross. THEREFORE . . .

(Col. 2:13–16)

Paul then explains the implications of the perfection of Christ's work for the Christian life. When we understand the cross, he says, and when we live in the light of it, we are planted in the soil in which we may grow in grace.
To the Corinthians he wrote:

Jews demand miraculous signs and Greeks look for wisdom, but we preach Christ crucified . . .

(1 Cor. 1:22)

Everything he says to the Corinthians to draw them back to the truth of the gospel is, in one way or another, an outworking and application of this mighty statement. If they are to grow they must be brought back to the cross.
To the Galatians he wrote:

May I never boast except in the cross of our Lord Jesus Christ, through which the world has been crucified to me, and I to the world.

(Gal. 6:14)

Clearly the cross lies at the heart of the gospel; it is the centre of everything else. Why should this be so? The answer is this: *we find grace through the cross and we grow in grace in proportion to the welcome we give to its implications.*

GRACE IN THE CROSS

In the New Testament 'the cross' has two different meanings. *It can mean an instrument of public execution*. The cross was a wooden structure on which a man was hung, bound to it with ropes and nails, until he died. Medical analyses and descriptions of the cause of death in the case of crucifixion leave a sickening feeling behind them. There is something indescribably degrading about such a mode of execution, matched only by the agony of the sufferer. In Jesus' case, as with so many others, he was already ruthlessly beaten, bruised and weakened before his crucifixion took place.

It was only to be expected that 'When all the people who had gathered to witness this sight saw what took place, they beat their breasts and went away' (Lk. 23:48), nor that the women of Jerusalem who saw him slowly make his way to Calvary 'mourned and wailed for him' (Lk. 23:27). Neither is it surprising that a Latin author could insist that even the name of the cross was not fit to be mentioned in decent Roman conversation.

Paul could never have 'boasted' in the cross if this was all it meant. If by preaching Christ crucified only this was involved, he was indeed of all men most miserable (see 1 Cor. 15:18).

But 'the cross' means something else. It not only an instrument of execution in the New Testament, but also *the means of our salvation*. When Paul preached 'the cross' he preached a message which explained that man's instrument of rejection had been used by God as his instrument of reconciliation. Man's means of bringing death to Jesus was God's means to bring life to the world. Man's symbol of rejecting Christ was God's symbol of forgiveness for man. This is why Paul boasted about the cross!

Now we must ask the all-important question: How do we find the grace of God in the cross? How has it become God's instrument of salvation to those who have faith? Paul's writings disclose no less than three reasons.

1. *The Cross of Christ demonstrates the love of God.* When the famous text John 3:16 tells us that God so loved the world that he *gave* his only Son that men might not perish it means that *God gave his Son over to the death of the cross.* The cross is the measure of the love of God. That is why James Denney, a Scottish theologian of a former generation, used to say that the only time he ever envied a Roman priest his crucifix was when he wanted to brandish one before his hearers and say: 'God loves you like that!'. Although he used no visual aid of that kind the apostle Paul saw this as the burden of his own preaching. We preach *Christ-having-been-crucified*, he said. Earlier, when lamenting the falling from grace of the Galatians (Gal. 5:4) he had reminded them of the nerve-centre of his own preaching:

> You foolish Galatians! Who has bewitched you? *Before your very eyes Jesus Christ was clearly portrayed as crucified.*
>
> (Gal. 3:1)

He spoke to them about Christ's work by way of personal testimony:

> The life I live in the body, I live by faith in the Son of God, *who loved me and gave himself for me.*
>
> (Gal. 2:20)

Again, in his letter to the Romans he had underlined the same thing—it is on the cross that we see the love of God demonstrated:

When we were still *powerless* Christ died for the *ungodly*.

God demonstrates his own love for us in this: *While we were still sinners, Christ died for us*.

When we were *God's enemies*, we were reconciled to him through the death of his Son.

(Rom. 5:6,8,10)

When we look at Christ dying on the cross we are shown the lengths to which God's love goes in order to win us back to himself. We would almost think that God loved us more than he loves his son! We cannot measure such love by any other standard. He is saying to us: I love you this much.

2. *The Cross demonstrates the justice of God*. Sometimes when we explain the message of the gospel to others we say something like this: 'God has laid aside his justice. He no longer deals with us as sinners; he forgets our sin, and accepts us'. But when we say this we distort the biblical teaching. For the New Testament's message is *not* 'God was in Christ reconciling the world to himself, not counting their tresspasses'. Rather it is: 'God was in Christ reconciling the world to himself, not counting their tresspasses *against them*'. Do you see the difference?

God did count our tresspasses. It is not on Mount Sinai that we discover this. There we hear God *telling us* what our tresspasses are, and that he will in no way pass by sin. But it is only on Mount

Calvary that we witness God counting men's sins, demonstrating his perfect justice. Yes, it is wonderfully true that he does not count our sins *against us*. But it is not the ultimate wonder. The wonder of all wonders is that *God counted our tresspasses against his Son the Lord Jesus Christ.* He did not pass them by; he punished them to the full in the person who 'himself bore our sins in his body on the tree' (1 Pet. 2:24). That was why Jesus cried out on the cross: 'My God, I am forsaken—why? why?' Heaven's answer was: 'Because you stand in the place of sinners; you bear their guilt; now you must sustain their punishment'. And so stroke upon stroke of divine judgment fell upon Jesus.

He was pierced for our transgressions,
   he was crushed for our iniquities;
the punishment that brought us peace was upon him,
   and by his wounds we are healed.
We all, like sheep, have gone astray,
   each of us has turned to his own way;
and the Lord has laid on him
   the iniquity of us all.

(Is. 53:5–6)

3. *The Cross demonstrates the wisdom of God.* How else could guilt and forgiveness appear in the presence of God at the same time? How else could God remain equally faithful to his love for us and his just judgment of our sins? The glory of the cross, its unimaginable wisdom lies in the way God has devised to provide salvation for his people:

> *O loving wisdom of our God*
> *When all was sin and shame*

> *A second Adam to the fight*
> *And to the rescue came.*
>
> *O wisest love, that flesh and blood*
> *Which did in Adam fail*
> *Should strive afresh against the foe*
> *Should strive and should prevail.*

It is truly the 'Trysting place where heaven's love and heaven's justice meet', as Horatius Bonar's great hymn puts it.

The cross therefore is the heart of the gospel. It is what makes the gospel good news: Christ has died for us. He has stood in our place before God's judgment seat. He has borne our sins. God has done something on the cross which we could never do for ourselves.

But God does something *to us* as well as *for us* through the cross. He provides us with the ultimate persuasion available to him that he does love us.

The view that the cross shows us the love of God is inadequate if taken on its own. Unfortunately that mistake has often been made. But when taken alongside what we have already seen it sheds important light on what we should discover when we look to Christ crucified. What God intends to do is to accept us for Christ's sake. But he wants to go further. It is in his heart to persuade us that he does accept us for Christ's sake. So he demonstrates, he gives adequate proof of his love to us. When I look at the cross, I too learn to say 'The Son of God *loved me*, and gave himself for me' (Gal. 2:20). I begin to believe with Paul that if God did not spare his own Son, but gave him up to the cross for me, then I know that he loves me so much he will always give me only what will bring me blessing (Rom. 8:32).

Such conviction is a key point in Christian growth. If we have deep-seated fears that God does not really love us (as many Christians have), we can only go so far in growing nearer to God. There will come a point at which we will fear to trust him any further because we cannot be sure of his love. At such a time our only hope is to sink ourselves and our fears into the grace he has revealed on the cross. When we look at ourselves, or our own faith, or our circumstances we will never be free from those lurking fears. Satan will see to that. But when we lift up our eyes and look on the cross we find the final persuasion that God is gracious towards us. How can he be against us when all his wrath against us fell upon Christ? How can he fail to care for us when he gave the only Son he had for our sakes? How can we doubt him when he has given us evidence of his love sufficient to banish all doubts?

The reason we lack assurance of his grace is because we fail to focus on that spot where he has revealed it. Fail to focus the eyes of our understanding there and we will fail to grow in grace.

There is however another aspect of the cross which we need to consider. It too is a critical point of growth for the child of God. Welcoming God's grace must be accompanied by a willingness to welcome with it all its implications. It was this Paul was thinking about when he said that he gloried in the cross *by which the world had been crucified to him and he to the world.* (Gal. 6:14).

THE IMPLICATIONS OF THE CROSS

1. *The world is crucified to the Christian.* Paul means 'the world' in the sense that it is estranged

from God, 'this age' dominated by sin.

He means 'the world' with its temptations, in all its insidious power to draw the Christian away from God.

What is to be done to the world in the Christian life? It is to be crucified. It is to receive the same treatment at the hands of the Christian as Jesus received at the hands of worldly men!

Paul also recognised that this relationship between the believer and the world is not natural. Crucifixion is not a natural death. It is a deliberate, public brutal execution. Nor can crucifixion be self-inflicted. The world does not go away on its own! It clings to us like a limpet, seeking to draw out of us all our spiritual powers. We must deal a mortal wound to its influence in our hearts and lives. Just as the Lord Jesus was an object of revulsion and rejection to the world, so it must be to us. Paul is saying the same thing here as Jesus. If our right eye, or hand causes us to sin, we should pluck it out or tear it off, he had said (Matt. 5:29–30). If we are to be his disciples we must deny self, take up the cross daily and follow him. There is no disharmony between our Lord and his apostle. The message is the same; the picture is one. Welcoming God's grace implies rejecting the world. Living for Christ means nothing less.

Why should this be so vital? It is a remarkable fact that so many practical issues like this one came under our Lord's scrutiny in his great parable of the Sower and the soils. He indicated to his disciples that in many ways it was the key to understanding all the other parables. It is almost impossible to write about the practicalities of being a Christian without coming back again and again to the principles which Jesus there teaches.

In this connection it is his description of the

thorny soil which is relevant. What did Jesus say? He emphasised that it is possible for growth to take place to a certain point, and then for fruitfulness to cease *because no weeding has been done in the heart*. In other words, no matter how much we build up the positive aspects of Christian character, unless we also deal radically with the remnants of indwelling sin in our lives, all will be lost. How foolish we are, when nature itself teaches us these lessons, and Jesus impresses them on us, to ignore the importance of dealing with a worldly spirit! The tragedy is that when we do nothing in this area of spiritual life we have provided exactly the conditions in which worldliness will grow. What a solemn warning! Paul expressed it perfectly to his friend Titus when he wrote:

> The grace of God that brings salvation has appeared to all men. It teaches us to say 'No' to ungodliness and worldly passions, and to live self-controlled, upright and godly lives in this present age, while we wait for the blessed hope—the glorious appearing of our great God and Saviour Jesus Christ, who gave himself for us to redeem us from all wickedness and to purify for himself a people that are his very own, eager to do what is good.

(Tit. 2:11–14)

What perfect balance! *The grace of God teaches us to say 'No'*.

2. *The Christian is crucified to the world.*
Some of us who recognise the necessity of the first implication of grace in our lives are stunned by the realism with which Paul speaks about this.

Our temptation is to draw back here. We are able to cope with the necessity of denying ourselves. Yet, find it difficult to accept that by yielding allegiance to Christ we are likely to be denied and rejected by others.

But the principle is an unavoidable one: 'in this world we are like him' (1 Jn. 4:17). Since he was a man of sorrows, despised and rejected by men, there will be times when we share in his suffering. That, for Paul was the sign of genuine sonship. We are heirs of God and joint heirs with Christ provided we suffer with him (Rom. 8:17). Paul himself bore *on his body* the marks of Jesus (Gal. 6:17).

There are times when crucifixion in the Christian's life is extended beyond inner spiritual experience. Paul spoke of how he filled up what was lacking, or remaining in the sufferings of Christ (Col. 1:24). He could go so far as to say that 'we always carry around in our body the death of the Lord Jesus . . . we . . . are always being given over to death for Jesus' sake' (2 Cor. 4:10–11).

What does this mean? It means that we must never forget—if we are to grow in grace, and therefore grow like Christ—that the One we trust, love and serve is a *crucified* Saviour. To follow him means taking up the cross, as well as denying ourselves. It means a crucified life!

At the end of chapter three we asked this question: Are you *willing* for all that is involved in growing spiritually? Now we have seen part of what is involved. Nothing less than the cross. Nothing less than saying with Paul that all we care for is to know Christ and the power of his resurrection, sharing the fellowship of his death, in order that we might attain to the resurrection from the dead (Phil. 3:10).

What, then, will you do about the cross, where God's grace is revealed, and where your will must bow to his?

We must do something about the cross, and one of two things only we can do—flee it or die upon it. And if we should be so foolhardy as to flee we shall by that act put away the faith of our fathers and make of Christianity something other than it is. Then we shall have left only the empty language of salvation; the power will depart with our departure from the true cross.

If we are wise we will do what Jesus did: endure the cross and despise its shame for the joy that is set before us. To do this is to submit the whole pattern of our lives to be destroyed and built again in the power of an endless life. And we shall find that it is more than poetry, more than sweet hymnody and elevated feeling. The cross will cut into our lives where it hurts worst, sparing neither us nor our carefully cultivated reputations. It will defeat us and bring our selfish lives to an end. Only then can we rise in fullness of life to establish a pattern of living wholly new and free and full of good works.

(A.W. Tozer, *The Root of the Righteous*, pp. 64–5)

> *Forbid it, Lord, that I should boast,*
> *Save in the death of Christ, my God;*
> *All the vain things that charm me most,*
> *I sacrifice them to his blood.*
>
> *Were the whole realm of Nature mine,*
> *That were an offering far too small;*
> *Love so amazing, so divine,*
> *Demands my soul, my life, my all.*

Isaac Watts.

SECTION THREE
LIFE TOGETHER

Christians are not isolationists. They do not exist on their own, but in groups, fellowships, communities known as 'churches'. This is the pattern which the Lord Jesus Christ laid down. He said 'I will build my church'.

What is the church for? One of its functions is to help us to grow in grace. How does it do this?

Sometimes it is in the context of Christian fellowship that some of the obstacles to true spiritual growth begin to appear. How can these be overcome?

6: Growing Together

Why did Jesus Christ die? We have already quoted Paul's words to Titus which emphasise that it was to 'purify for himself a people that are his very own' (Tit. 2:14). When we looked at this verse before it was to stress the necessity of learning to say 'no' if we are to grow in grace. What we must now notice is that Paul emphasises here and in many other places, that Christ wants to create 'a people', not merely isolated individuals who believe in him.

The story of God's work throughout the Old Testament underlines the same point. Always God is interested in and working through individuals. But he does so because he is concerned to call together a nation of men and women who serve him and witness to his glory throughout the earth. In this chapter and the next we must give more careful consideration to what this means in terms of our own spiritual development.

Paul describes the church as a building, a temple. Christ is the cornerstone. The ministry of the apostles and prophets serves as the foundation. In Christ 'the whole building is joined together and rises to become a holy temple in the Lord' (Eph. 2:20). God is not only shaping us to be like Christ; he is shaping us in such a way that we should *fit together*. In order to reflect Christ more perfectly our relationships with our fellow Christians must be developed!

This is so obvious, and yet we frequently overlook its importance. The more firmly we are held in place by the chief cornerstone, the more securely we will be bound together with the other stones in the building. We can learn the same lesson from the picture of the church as the flock over which Christ is set as the Chief Shepherd. When he calls his sheep and they respond to his voice, they are brought closer to him. But as he welcomes them to himself they inevitably are drawn closer to each other!

Our lives are intended by God to be ministries to the lives of our fellow Christians. We ought to be able to say to our fellow Christians:

I will continue with all of you *for your progress and joy in the faith*' (Phil. 1:25). If this is to be so, there are several features of the New Testament's teaching we will need to appreciate.

YOUR MINISTRY TO OTHERS

Every Christian has a gift. The Spirit gives one to each person, just as he determines (1 Cor. 12:11). What is this gift for? 'To each one the manifestation of the Spirit is given *for the common good*' (1 Cor. 12:7). These are illuminating words indeed. A gift, Paul suggests, is a manifestation of the Spirit'. It is a means by which the Spirit shows us more of Christ. He does so by using some ability he has given us in the service of others.

Martin Luther used to speak about the Christian being 'a little Christ' to his neighbour. That is what Paul means here. Unlike many of us, Paul did not think of a gift of the Spirit as something which makes the recipient seem special or important. A gift of the Spirit is meant to show that Christ is special. The only person the Spirit wants to manifest is Jesus! (See Jn. 16:12–14 and Jn. 14:21,23) When we exercise the gifts which

Christ has given us we are really saying to our fellow Christians and others: *See how much the Lord Jesus Christ loves you and cares for you*; he has sent me to love you and serve you in this way; he is using my hands and feet, my lips and ears, to show his love in this special way. It is a tragic mistake if we think that the message is: See what a super Christian I am; see the wonderful gifts I have.

The point was well illustrated in the Upper Room. While Jesus' disciples were arguing with one another about which one of them was the greatest and had the best gifts (how like the Corinthians!), Jesus was thinking: How can I show these disciples that gifts are not for ourselves but for others? The outcome, of course, was the washing of the disciples' feet. *Gifts are for service*. We belong to each other (Rom. 12:5); we need each other to reflect the fulness of the love of Christ (1 Cor. 12:21). We must therefore learn to see the gifts we have received as instruments by which we can love and serve others.

These general considerations help us to make sense of Paul's statement in Ephesians 4:11ff that 'Christ gave some (gifts to the church) . . . so that the body of Christ may be built up until we all . . . become mature'. Maturity, spiritual manhood is the *raison d'etre* of your spiritual gifts and mine. This was the driving force in Paul's ministry: 'so that we may present everyone perfect (literally, *mature*) in Christ. To this end I labour, struggling with all his energy, which so powerfully works in me' (Col. 1:28–9). But Paul is not unique in this respect. He may have possessed more gifts or different gifts from the ones we do (and certainly he had many gifts); but his aim and ours must be one. We live in Christian fellowship for this important function in one another's lives—so that we may serve each other with our gifts and thus promote true spiritual growth in the body of Christ.

If we are to put this teaching into practice we must have a proper appreciation of what Christ's gifts are, and how they are related to each other in the fellowship of the church.

THE NATURE OF OUR GIFTS

What we call 'spiritual gifts' (*pneumatika*) are also known in the New Testament as 'grace gifts' (*charismata*). They are manifestations of the Spirit, but they are never to be thought of apart from the grace of the Lord Jesus Christ and the graciousness he produces in the lives of his children. We should never confuse the gifts of the Spirit with the grace or fruit of the Spirit. However the gifts of the Spirit are meant *to produce* the fruit of the Spirit in our and others' lives. They are given to the church by the risen, ascended and reigning Lord Jesus Christ for this purpose. Just as when a king celebrates his coronation, gifts are given to his people in unusual ways, so the gifts which Christ has given to his church are symbols of his coronation. Like a Roman general returning home in triumph 'he led captives in his train and gave gifts to me' (Eph. 4:8). When we receive these gifts; when we employ them for others' blessing; when we receive help through others' gifts, we should recognise that Jesus is Lord, that he reigns and has been crowned. We have become the recipients of his royal bounty.

But if the first thing to recognise is that spiritual gifts are given to us from Christ through the Spirit, we must further realise that they are all related to the word of God.

In the different lists which the New Testament gives of the gifts of Christ to the church it is noticeable that the 'greater' gifts (1 Cor. 12:31) are those which are most obviously tied to the ministry of the word of God in some form or another. Apostles were the channels of it to the whole church of God in every age; prophets were mouthpieces of it and applied it particularly to contemporary situations; pastors and teachers used it in order to build up the local congregations in their faith. Words of wisdom and knowledge obviously fed upon its truth and it served as the background to their usefulness; tongues and their interpretation grew richer through familiarity with it, and were tested by it; miracles, healings, helps, and all other gifts witnessed to its truth and power to save. Because the character of our service and its quality, whatever our gift, depends on the kind of men and women we are, so those gifts depended on that special divine instrument which moulds and shapes Christian character—the word of God.

It is essential for us to realise, especially in the climate of our modern church, that God's word is the central gift Christ gives to the church. The major gifts of the New Testament era were given either to write that word (apostles), apply it (prophets) or teach it (pastors and teachers). Whenever we dislocate our own spiritual gift from this anchor we begin to flounder in a sea of uncertainty and instability. We must see to it that our gifts are fed on the teaching of Holy Scripture, so that they grow strong and are channelled in the right direction, and so bring glory to Christ. But how, precisely is this to be achieved?

PRODUCING GROWTH

Paul tells us that these fundamental ministries of the church were given by Christ 'to prepare God's people for works of service' (Eph. 4:12). It is in this way that the body of Christ is built up to maturity. These ministries are meant to help us to exercise our ministry. The purpose of each gift is to promote the use of all the other gifts.

This is why Paul was so attracted by the picture of the church as the body of Christ and individual Christians as particular members. The whole body needs the eye, if it is to function properly. But it also needs the parts which Paul describes as 'less honourable' (1 Cor. 12:23). Failure to function properly in any area means that the body is not able to function properly (Eph. 4:16). Failure to grow in one member distorts the usefulness of the whole.

The word Paul uses in Ephesians 4:12 is a most interesting one. Although it is translated by 'prepare' in the NIV, it is the same word which is used in the Gospels of the disciples 'mending' their nets and 'preparing' them for the next night's fishing. The picture is of them restoring broken and frayed parts of the nets, and folding them in readiness for service later on. Later in 2 Timothy 3:16–17, when he is discussing the effect of God's word in the life of the believer, Paul uses very similar language: God's word prepares us for every good work. This is a marvellous illustration of what the basic ministry of God's word is meant to accomplish in our lives. God means to use it to get us in readiness to employ the gifts he has given to us. In turn our gifts will help others to use the gifts which he has given to them. In this way, as we serve one another in Christian fellowship, the momentum of our usefulness increases. We grow in grace and in the knowledge of the Lord Jesus Christ.

This always has a twofold effect, both negative and positive.

Negative effects

'Then we will no longer be infants' (Eph. 4:14). Paul appealed to the Corinthians to let the word of God produce this kind of effect in their lives: Do not be children, but adults, in the way you think (1 Cor. 14:20).

Infants are always unsteady on their feet. They are usually attracted by appearances. The items which are available for sale in a baby shop illustrate the point. You will need to buy a large fireguard; a special door gate; covers for electric points; a play pen—to name but a few of the items which will keep an infant safe! Infants need to be protected from the harm they are likely to do to themselves as much as anything else. They lack experience and understanding, inevitably. They are not to be criticised for that! But they do need to be protected because of it. The time comes, however, when they should have gained sufficient experience and understanding to be able to find their way in life, step by step. They come to see that while fire is attractive it burns; that while electricity is a wonderful servant it is a deadly master; that house stairs are for walking up, not for tumbling down!

The same is true for the young Christian. He is unsteady. He does not naturally possess the discernment necessary to steer his path through the false teaching, the subtle temptations, the many snares which he meets. Any wind of doctrine may blow him over and carry him along in its wake. The first essential is to enable him to stand. The only way this can be achieved is by gaining the understanding of God's word and ways which will safeguard him. This is always the first benefit we receive as young Christians from the ministry of others. There is a protecting and stabilising influence in the teaching we receive from the word of God.

Positive effects

Instead of being tossed about as infants, the ministry of others brings stability. It also produces growth in love: 'Instead, speaking the truth *in love*, we will in all things grow up into him who is the Head, that is, Christ. From him the whole body, joined and held together by every supporting ligament, grows and builds itself up *in love*, as each part does its work.' (Eph. 4:15–16).

The promotion and practice of love is fundamental to all spiritual growth. The church is built up by love, and is a community which has learned to 'speak the truth in love'. Paul literally says that we 'truth-in-love'. We have no equivalent verb 'to truth'. He means much more than 'speaking the truth'. Illustrate, express, demonstrate the truth in love, is what he means. There is a reality and a transparency which should develop in a Christian fellowship where the gifts of the Spirit are exercised in the proper way. The aim of Paul's own ministry was precisely this: 'the goal . . . is love' he wrote to Timothy (1 Tim. 1:5).

John Owen, a famous Puritan preacher, once explained the importance of love in a Christian fellowship in this way. The church, he said, is like a bundle of sticks—some long, some short; some straight, some bent; some fat, some thin. We have different interests, personalities, backgrounds, spheres of life. What do you do if you want to carry a bundle of sticks of different shapes and sizes? You bind them together in a bundle. One piece of rope makes the task straightforward. So too in the church of Christ. There is only one thing which will hold together such diverse groupings of people—and so Paul says: 'put on love, which binds . . . all together in perfect unity' (Col. 3:14).

But how is this love produced by the use of the gifts God has given to his people? We have already seen the answer. It lies partly in the fact that gifts are given to us so that we can serve others, so that we can show Christ's love and our own love for them. But the answer also lies in the influence these gifts have on our lives. They teach us why we should love one another, because God has loved us. They teach us why we should welcome and forgive one another, because Christ has welcomed and forgiven us (Rom. 15:7; Eph. 4:32). The ministry of God's word, in particular, should open up to us the great wonders of the gospel, and lead us to yield ourselves at an ever deepening level to the service of the Lord Jesus Christ and all who belong to him.

What then should we look for in our Christian fellowships? What should we pray for is they are to be communities in which the body of Christ upbuilds itself in love?

We should look first of all for a ministry of God's word. It is clear from what we have seen in Paul's teaching that while this is not the only gift which Christ has given to the church (nor for that matter does it seem to have been the exclusive province of only one person in each New Testament congregation), it remains the central gift. All other gifts depend and feed on it.

The ministry of the word builds us up. It does so through the instruction it gives to our minds and the way in which it shapes our thinking. Through its influence we learn the truths and principles which help us to love God more, to appreciate our fellow Christians and to understand the will of God for our lives. The ministry of the word also protects us against harmful teaching and influences. Through its effect on us we learn to distinguish between what is true and what is false, what is real and what is counterfeit. According to Peter, growing in grace and the knowledge of Christ *is always contrasted* with being 'carried away by the error of lawless men' and so falling from our secure position in Christ (2 Pet. 3:17–18). It remains the central necessity in all Christian fellowship.

The ministry of the word is intended to produce a fellowship of love, as we have also seen. There will be a mutual serving of one another in the life-style of God's gathered people. There will be a reflection of Christ who came among us as 'one who serves' (Lk. 22:7). That love will at times express itself in a willingness to suffer with each other and for one another. Paul, who said that if one member suffers the whole body will suffer, who stressed that we should weep with those who weep, also spoke about being willing to suffer in the place of his fellow Christians (1 Cor. 12:26; Rom. 12:15; Col. 1:24). That is always the fruit of love, and it must be so in our fellowships too.

Love also means caring for the needy, for love is nothing if it is not really practical. Love is always simple rather than complicated, caring rather than merely demonstrative. Consequently the teaching of the Bible about spiritual growth includes exhortations to use our time, talents and financial resources in the interests of others. Indeed, true spiritual growth, modelled on Christ's life, means looking out for the interests and needs of others rather than our own.

We grow through Christian fellowship too because it is the context in which we witness for Christ. We cannot reflect the whole of Jesus in our own lives. We need all of our fellow-Christians to be able to show his grace and power. People will only see a fragment of all that Christ is able to do when they look at us. But when they are drawn into the fellowship to which we belong, then they may find how fully Christ is able to save and keep those who trust in him. They will recognise that our witness to Christ is much more than merely a different standard of living. It is rather the direct result of the presence of Christ in our lives and among his people.

The Christians of many centuries ago used to say that 'there is no salvation outside of the church'. Their words are open to misunderstanding, but when we properly understand them they are full of biblical truth. You cannot be a Christian in isolation; you cannot grow by shutting yourself off from contact with fellow disciples; you cannot adequately receive the help God intends to give you, or properly share the love of Christ. 'In Christ we who are many form one body, *and each member belongs to all the others*' (Rom. 12:5). Christ has given us gifts in order to serve each other and to witness to his glory, '*until we all reach unity in the faith and in the knowledge of the Son of God and become mature, attaining to the whole measure of the fulness of Christ*' (Eph. 4:13).

7: Restricted Growth

God's purpose, as we have now seen in general terms, is that we should grow as Christians in the context of Christian fellowship. We need one another in order to show all the facets of what Peter calls the 'multi-coloured' grace of God (1 Pet. 4:10). We need one another in order to receive the rich variety of blessing which Christ intends to give to us through our fellow Christians.

But when we look realistically at our Christian fellowships, we are forced to acknowledge that being together causes as many problems as it seems to solve! We come to recognise that the church is a community in which we receive spiritual help, but also one in which deep-seated problems will come to the surface and will require treatment. When we enter hospital for a check-up we may have very minor symptoms; but after we have been there a little time the consultant may say to us: 'It is just as well you came here when you did, because we have diagnosed a more serious illness, and we will now be able to treat you for that too'. Similarly, in Christian fellowship, through the ministry of the word of God, through the care of our fellow-believers, we often discover things about our own hearts and needs which we never anticipated.

So, there is a positive way to look at the problems which inevitably arise in every fellowship. But that does not diminish the seriousness of these problems.

In chapter four we mentioned that one of the churches which proved to be a burden on Paul's spirit was the one at Corinth. They seemed to have received so many blessings. They had been 'enriched in every way' (2 Cor. 2:12) in Christ (1 Cor. 1:5). Paul's testimony to the ascended Christ had been confirmed in Corinth through the presence of many spiritual gifts. They eagerly waited for the return of Christ (1 Cor. 1:7). Yet they simultaneously had many signs of spiritual immaturity. Paul's first letter to them reveals that there were many practical and doctrinal questions still being discussed by the Corinthians the answers to which should have been settled in their minds long beforehand. Paul wanted to speak to them as spiritual men, but he was discovering in a painful way that they were 'mere infants'. He could only give them milk, because they were still not ready for solid food (1 Cor. 3:1–2). There was jealousy and quarrelling among them. They were acting like ordinary men and women rather than as the children of God. Paul could well believe that there were divisions among them (1 Cor. 11:18). Maturity had been given a back seat. All the signs of childishness were returning. The situation was critical.

In the second letter to these Christians Paul continued to wrestle with this problem. He put his finger on one of the issues which was stunting their spiritual advance. He appealed to them *by name* (something he did very rarely). He expressed himself as best he knew how in these words:

We have spoken freely to you, Corinthians, and opened wide our hearts to you. We are not withholding our affection from you, but you are withholding yours from us. As a fair exchange—I speak as to my children—open wide your hearts also.

2 Corinthians 6:11–13

The Corinthians were suffering from a narrowing of their spiritual heart-arteries. In natural life the whole quality of life is impaired by such a condition. So in spiritual things growth is stunted and the quality of our Christian experience impoverished. The symptom of their sickness, in this case, was *the nature of their relationship with a fellow Christian*—with the apostle Paul. The rich warm blood of affection and love was no longer flowing through the body of Christ at Corinth with its former freedom and fulness. We learn from their experience that a closed heart is a major cause of lack of spiritual growth. Only an open heart towards our fellow Christians makes for authentic and natural spiritual development.

A CLOSED HEART

There are many signs of the needy spiritual condition of the Christians at Corinth, and particularly of how closed their hearts had grown to their fellow Christian, Paul. Before they had welcomed him and rejoiced in the ministry which he was able to offer to them. Now things had dramatically changed. One of the most obvious of these symptoms of decay is the number of times Paul uses the idea of recommendation or commendation. It appears more frequently in 2 Corinthians than in the rest of the New Testament put together!

What did this mean? Paul had earlier asked the church:

Are we beginning to commend ourselves again?
Or do we need, like some people, letters of
recommendation to you or from you?

2 Corinthians 3:1

To cut a long story short, Paul had become what
we sometimes call *persona non grata*. He was no
longer welcome among the Corinthians the way
he had formerly been. Apparently some of them
were beginning to ask: 'Who is he, anyway? What
right does he have to a special place in our hearts?
What authority does he have?'

There is no doubt that this situation caused
Paul great heartache. He felt like a parent whose
children have turned their backs on him, refusing
to confide their secrets, and worse, refusing to
share their lives to any degree. It is interesting to
notice that Paul speaks about his relationship
with the Corinthians in these precise terms (1
Cor. 4:15; 2 Cor. 6:13; 12:14–15). The hearts that
were once most open to us are often those which
become most tightly closed when their affection
is withdrawn. In this case the great principles of
growth within the body of Christ which Paul
describes in Ephesians 4 had ceased to operate.
From some points of view the condition gave all
the signs of being terminal. The situation was
highly critical.

Yet, the church at Corinth tells a story which is
repeated in miniature in many fellowships, and in
the hearts of many individual Christians. Fellowship is blocked, growth ceases, the light of grace
and love no longer shines as it once did. What are
the causes of this? Two stand out in the case of the
Corinthians.

1. *Because of their own lack of spiritual discernment the Corinthians had been estranged from*

Paul's affection by the influence of others. If you sit down and read through the letters to Corinth, particularly the second one, you will begin to feel that Paul seems to be looking over the shoulders of the Corinthians in what he writes. Of course his comments are directed towards them, but they also show an acute awareness of the influence of others on the Corinthians. For example, Paul contrasts his own ministry with that of 'others':

Unlike so many, we do not peddle the word of God for profit.

Do we need, *like some people*, letters of recommendation to you or from you?

2 Corinthians 2:17; 3:1

Who were these 'so many'? Who were these 'some people' about whom Paul was writing? Eventually Paul brings them out into the open:

We do not dare to classify or compare ourselves with some who commend themselves.

But I do not think I am in the least inferior to those 'super-apostles'.

For such men are false apostles, deceitful workmen, masquerading as apostles of Christ . . . Their end will be what their actions deserve.

2 Corinthians 10; 12; 11:5,13

Here were men who had followed Paul in the church at Corinth and had wormed their way into the confidence of the people by making a great boast of their gifts and message. But they seem to have abused God's word, sought their own personal gain and were a harmful influence. In order to establish their own authority they found it necessary to play down the authority of the apostle Paul, to oppose his teaching, and most of all, to turn sour the former affection which these young Christians had felt towards him. Now, they were told, their 'apostle' had feet of clay. He was able to use words well when he wrote, but he was lacking in eloquence in person (2 Cor. 10:10); he had many faults . . . and where did he get his authority from in any case? The Corinthians were too immature and lacking in discernment to understand what was happening to them. But Paul was in no doubt. Satan masquerades sometimes as a messenger of light, he said, and we should not be surprised if his servants do likewise (2 Cor. 11:13–15).

There is something really alarming about this situation. For these Corinthians were the same people who, previously, had caused Paul so much trouble with their party-spirit. They had grouped themselves around a favourite preacher—Paul, or Apollos, or Peter. They had been far more interested in the individual presentation of the gospel message than with the message itself. They had not distinguished between what was merely the outward and secondary matter of the messenger, and the inner, central matter of the truth of God.

Are we surprised to discover that these same people who lacked spiritual discernment in that context (where the same truth was being preached by these three faithful stewards of the gospel) also lacked discernment when they were the recipients of false teaching and under the influence of false teachers? Whenever they saw great talents, outward pomp and show, they followed. It did not much matter to them what tune was being played, so long as some pied piper was playing it! They would follow wherever he led.

Over and over again this happens in the church. Christians begin to grow in grace. But then they are swept off their feet by some new movement, some novel teaching, or organisation—something bigger, better, more exciting, seemingly more spiritual. One of the symptoms is that our hearts begin to close to Christians who previously meant so much to us, from whom we received help over long periods of time. Their care was humble, constant, faithful. But now it is seen to have been totally lacking in what we really needed! It is the radical nature of the change of heart that we should find so disturbing. It is so reminiscent of the Israelites during the wilderness wanderings, complaining, murmuring against Moses. We need to learn as early as we can in Christian experience to have a healthy suspicion of any influence in our lives which begins to close our hearts to those who have been a spiritual help to us. That is not the kind of work of which the Spirit of God is the author.

This reaction to Paul and his ministry was not unaccompanied by other alarming trends in the church at Corinth. It rarely is.

2. *The Corinthians were also, apparently, refusing to rid their lives of known sin.* In many translations there is a marked gap between the end of 2 Corinthians 6:13 and 14. Paul is now taking up a new theme. But it is vital to notice that the issue to which he turns is integrally related to what he has just been discussing. His appeal to the

Corinthians to open their hearts to him is followed by a summons to live a life of holiness:

What do righteousness and wickedness have in common?
What fellowship can light have with darkness?
What harmony is there between Christ and Belial?
What does a believer have in common with an unbeliever?
What agreement is there between the temple of God and idols?

2 Corinthians 6:14–16

All this leads up to his great exhortation to self-purification, 'perfecting holiness out of reverence for God' (2 Cor. 7:1).

Why this sudden attack on sin? The reason is not difficult to imagine. Did Paul suspect, or even definitely know that the Corinthians were living lives of double standards, professing Christ (according to the new 'light' they had received from the false teachers), yet living in fellowship with known sin? Was this why they had begun to turn away from Paul and the ministry he exercised, why they began to propagate criticism about him? Was this the only way they could justify the double standard in their lives? Were they accusing Paul of an inconsistency ('his letters are weighty, but in person he amounts to nothing' 2 Cor. 10:10) to hide the depths of their own inconsistency?

There is a good deal of evidence in the Corinthian correspondence to suggest that this was the case. It should not come as a shock to us that it was. We find the same characteristics present in the Pharisees. Why did they attack Jesus? What possible motive lay behind their accusations of inconsistency in his life? It was surely the fact that his ministry was uncovering the truth about many of them, and was exposing the sin in their hearts. Jesus' life and ministry demonstrated that while they had separated themselves from outward immorality, many of them were self-seeking, grace-abandoning enemies of God (See Matt. 23:13ff): The only way of self-defence was to attack Christ. So in Corinth. There could be no 'peace' in the conscience until the teaching and gracious influence of Paul had been silenced there.

There is a great difference between a necessary spiritual and biblical discernment of error and a spirit of criticism towards a fellow Christian. We are encouraged to exercise the first. But the second is a poison which will eventually destroy us. It is a sign that growth has ceased.

Sometimes we think that sin in our lives is entirely a private matter, between the individual and God. In a sense that is true. But sin can never be kept within these bounds, especially in the life of the professing Christian. Sooner or later it breaks out. It shows its true colours—for it always takes the shape of antagonism against grace, either in Christ himself or in his disciples. In the case of the Corinthians the tell-tale sign was antagonism against Paul. What concerned Paul was the fact that antagonism against Christ himself was the next logical step.

That is a warning which we need to heed.

What is to be done when spiritual growth is thus hindered? In a nutshell what this passage is teaching us is: Do not be like the Corinthians; be like the apostle Paul. What, therefore, can we learn from him?

AN OPEN HEART OF FELLOWSHIP

The natural thing for Paul to have done in this situation was to have closed his heart against the Corinthians. Tit-for-tat! This is the way of the world, and it is often our way, despite our fellowship in Christ's church.

I remember as a child listening to school radio programmes of music and action. We would stand in our seats, and when the announcer told us 'You are a flower' and the music played, we pretended to be just that—flowers! We opened up as the sun rose in the sky, and then closed down as sunset came and it was time for flowers to go back to bed! Yes, we were flowers alright! But there is more than a grain of truth in that thought. For we do respond to warmth and appreciation—it brings us out of ourselves. We are drawn to those who take an interest in us. We tend to close up in our spirits when we feel others do not accept us, or when we find their reactions cold toward us.

The extraordinary feature of Paul was that *the more the hearts of the Corinthians were closed to him, the more he opened his heart to them*. Whereas they had spoken behind his back, he said 'We have spoken freely to you'. Whereas they had narrowed their hearts towards him, he had 'opened wide' his heart to them. Whereas they had withheld their affection from him, he had not withheld his from them. *This is true growth in grace*. It is seen in two ways in this strained relationship between Paul and these Christians.

1. *Paul's confession of personal weakness*. We noticed in the previous chapter that one of the fruits of spiritual growth in the context of fellowship is reality in love.

Paul had been accused of weakness. So he confessed his many weaknesses, and the occasions on which he had been most conscious of them. He said: God has put the treasure of the gospel in jars of clay which are easily broken; such are we (2 Cor. 4:7). He illustrated the point: 'We do not want you to be uninformed, brothers, about the hardships we suffered in the province of Asia. We were under great pressure, far beyond our ability to endure, *so that we despaired even of life*' (2 Cor. 2:8). Again, speaking of his previous correspondence, 'I wrote you out of great distress and anguish of heart and with many tears, not to grieve you but to let you know the depth of my love for you' (2 Cor. 2:4). Hardly the words of a man who gave himself out to be an impregnable leader!

But perhaps even more remarkable is his confession in 2 Corinthians 2:12-13. The Lord had opened a door for him to preach the gospel in Troas. But he did not find his friend Titus there. He became anxious and left. In short, he had an outstanding evangelistic opportunity given to him, but he failed to rise to the occasion because he was overcome with worry about a friend. We do not here need to assess the seriousness of Paul's failure. All we need to see is that he confessed that he had failed his Lord as an evangelist. Furthermore, if 2 Corinthians 4:1 and 16 give an accurate reflection of Paul's own experience it seems that there were many times in his ministry when he was in grave danger of losing heart, and had needed to resist the temptation by anchoring himself to the great truths of the gospel.

Why all this personal confession? After all there was another dimension altogether to the character and ministry of Paul—his driving ambition to serve Christ; his long list of successful periods and places of service; his great strength of mind and the special revelation he had received—why then did he not beat the Corinthians with an apostolic stick (as he himself had suggested was a possibility open to him, 1 Cor. 4:21). Why come to them in such evident weakness?

The answer is straightforward. Which would be the more Christ-like? Which would show the affection he continued to feel for the Corinthians? Which would most clearly prove that he was concerned for them and not merely for his own position? Which was the more likely to win them back to the 'meekness and gentleness of Christ' (2 Cor. 10:1)?

Alexander Whyte, the famous minister of Free St. George's Church in Edinburgh, said, many decades ago, that there is such a thing as sanctification by vinegar. What did he mean? When we were children we used to play a game called 'Conkers'. We bored a hole through a chestnut, and suspended it from a piece of string with a knot in the end. The idea of the game was to take alternate swipes at one another's chestut. Proud was the boy who won in successive games, destroying his opponent's conker on each occasion. Having a 'tenner' (a conker undefeated in ten successive matches) was an achievement in itself. But sometimes we would become suspicious of a friend's success. 'You've used vinegar!' the accusation would be made. That was cheating—soaking the chestnut in vinegar to make it specially hard.

Some Christians live their Christian lives in that way. They become unloving, unyielding, 'holy' in a formal, critical, unattractive way. They have a holiness (it would be better to say 'rectitude') without love. They have 'been sanctified by vinegar', not by grace. But nobody has ever been drawn closer to the Saviour, restored from rebellion and sin, by such a Christian. Only grace can restore. That was why Paul shared with the Corinthians his own need of grace, and the welcome which Christ's grace in his life would give to them.

Do you know anything of that kind of costly spiritual growth?

2. *Paul's application of God's grace.* In the previous section of this letter Paul had been explaining the nature of God's saving grace. God was reconciling the world to himself in the death of his Son. Now God appealing through Paul's ministry: Be reconciled to God. His work was to invite people to receive God's grace. His message was evangelistic (2 Cor. 5:14ff). But when he turns to this new theme in chapter 6, he is simply making a pastoral application of the same basic message. He urges the Corinthians 'not to receive God's reconciling grace in vain' (2 Cor. 6:1).

What does Paul mean? He saw the contradiction inherent in a group of people who claimed to be reconciled to God but refused to be reconciled to Paul. He is urging those who have received reconciliation in Christ to display that reconciliation in their relationships with others.

Whenever we close up our hearts against a fellow Christian we are also closing them up against God. We are refusing to allow his grace to produce its fruit in our hearts. For grace has been offered to us to make us gracious to others.

The testimony of the apostle John echoes that of Paul:

If anyone says 'I love God' yet hates his brother, he is a liar. For anyone who does not love his brother, whom he has seen, cannot love God, whom he has not seen. And he has given us this commandment: Whoever loves God must love his brother.

1 John 4:20-1

If we fail to open our hearts to our brothers and sisters in Christ, we are failing to open them to Christ. If we fail here then we cease to grow in true grace.

But how do we open our hearts to our brothers; how do we grow in grace in the context of our fellowship with one another? Paul's answer lies in what he had already said about not receiving the grace of God in vain. The way to open our hearts to others is by receiving afresh the grace of God and appreciating what it means: seeing our own need of Christ; coming to receive his mercy; sensing how undeserved his love for us is; remembering how he opened his heart to those whose hearts were closed against us. Then we will see that the heart which is too narrow to receive a fellow Christian is too narrow to enthrone the Lord Jesus Christ. But the heart that is opened to receive the grace of Christ will learn to welcome all those whom Christ himself has welcomed.

And this is my prayer: that your love may abound more and more . . .

Philippians 1:9

SECTION FOUR
CASE HISTORIES

Most of us find it an encouragement in our own Christian growth to learn what God has done in the lives of others. We learn not only by direct instruction, but by example and illustration.

This is why the Bible is more than a handbook to the Christian life. It is also full of biographical accounts of men and women who grew in grace.

Growth comes through our faithfulness. Growth sometimes comes through a crisis. Growth also comes through the pastoral counsel and encouragement of others.

Each of these paths to spiritual maturity is reflected in the lives of one or other of God's servants in Scripture. In this section three of them are singled out as 'case-studies' in Christian growth.

8: Daniel—Growing Faithfully

I still remember curling up in bed as a child on a cold winter morning, with my grandmother's old, thick page, small print Bible. There were two stories to which I most frequently turned in the Old Testament, although I had some difficulty finding both of them! I loved the story of Joseph—but sometimes as a very young boy forgot that there was no Book of Joseph! Even more taxing on my patience was leafing through from Genesis to find the Book of Daniel. It was a special favourite.

It was much later that I first heard the words of the well known chorus:

> *Dare to be a Daniel*
> *Dare to stand alone*
> *Dare to have a purpose firm*
> *Dare to make it known.*

Those are certainly some of the outstanding characteristics of Daniel's life. Even among biblical characters he stands out as an example of true loyalty and devotion to God. Unlike so many other men and women whose biographies are recorded in Scripture, he was a man of apparently consistent integrity. He was without obvious blemish. He is set before us as a model of spiritual life and growth.

In particular Daniel is singled out in the Bible

for two characteristics: righteousness and faith. His name became synonymous with righteousness, like Noah and Job (see Ezek. 14:20). His faith as one who 'shut the mouths of lions' is impressed upon us as an example to follow (see Heb. 11:33).

Yet, perhaps the most impressive thing about Daniel is his consistency. Like so many other saints he doubtless had his inward trials and struggles. He certainly faced very considerable opposition to the stand he took for God. But through it all he faithfully and patiently continued to grow in grace and in the knowledge of God. We can fairly safely assume that, provided we can glean enough personal information about his life, he can teach us a great deal about the basic lessons of growing up to full manhood as a child of God.

Of course we do not all grow like Daniel. God's ways with us may be quite different in their outworking. We shall see in the lives of others in the following chapters that God did not deal with every single saint in biblical times according to a stereotyped pattern. But, for all the different applications of God's purposes, we discover that the basic principles of true spiritual growth remain the same. From each person whose biography God has recorded in his word we should try to learn something for our own lives. In this way Daniel is a particularly helpful model.

There are four aspects of his growth which we should seek to imitate. For young Christians the first of them is one of the most vital lessons we can ever learn.

'Dare to be a Daniel!' But what was so daring about him? We all know what it was. If there are two things you know about him they are that he spent the night in a lions' den, and that 'Daniel resolved not to defile himself with the royal food and wine' (Dan. 1:8).

The important point is not what it was which he regarded as defiling. It is the general principle which he had adopted: nothing which defiles, that is, *nothing which will incur the displeasure of the Lord will ever have any place in my life*. That is the principle which we earlier saw lying close to the heart of 'the fear of God'. God's smile was the most important thing in Daniel's life and the guiding principle of all his behaviour. He therefore resolved that he would always do what was pleasing to his heavenly Father. That is the only solid foundation, the only water-tight principle of Christian living on which we can ever build a useful Christian life. Unless we are single minded here we will be unstable in all our ways (cf. Jas. 1:8).

What did this mean in practical terms for Daniel? How did he bring this theory down into actual nitty-gritty practice? Take the case of the food and drink he was offered. How did he apply this principle of wholehearted commitment to the Lord in that situation?

Daniel recognised that spiritual growth depends on two things: first a willingness to live according to the word of God; second, a willingness to take whatever consequences emerge as a result. There was almost certainly nothing wrong with the king's food. The very reverse would have been true—it was the best that money could buy.

But Daniel was convinced that, by the standard of God's revealed word, it would have been a defilement on his spirit to accept it. He realised that he could not say that he loved God with all his heart and soul and strength, but at the same time engage in pursuits which dishonoured him. In the case of the food and drink he was offered, it had in all probability been dedicated to an idol—the 'grace' said before it was eaten would have been in the form of a prayer of thanksgiving to a false god. To take the food, Daniel believed, was tantamount to denying his Lord and Master.

From one point of view, as doubtless many of his companions told him, Daniel's attitude must have appeared prejudiced and narrow! Could he not just enjoy the food and continue to believe in God inwardly? Why make so much fuss about a plate of food?

That is often the difference in perspective between the man who lives by sight and the man who lives by faith. One man sees only food; the other sees beyond the food to the face and presence and will of his Father in heaven. He sees that in every action he is either proclaiming or denying his loyalty to his Lord. Daniel was presumably relatively indifferent to the food itself; but he could never be indifferent to God's honour. Because he believed that the ultimate issue was the honour of God, he declined to eat and drink. He was faithful to his resolution. He recognised that, to borrow an apt phrase from A. W. Tozer, 'Some things are not negotiable'. He would therefore take his stand on God's word and take the consequences.

Three features of this decision on Daniel's part should be carefully noted by everyone who wishes to make spiritual progress.

(i) *Daniel, like Caleb before him, followed the Lord wholeheartedly* (Deut. 1:36). Scripture makes definite promises to wholeheartedness (Jer. 24:7; 29:13). Without it we shall never grow in any marked way in the knowledge of God. Only when we yield ourselves unreservedly to him can we say that he is truly our Lord.

William Booth, the founder of the Salvation Army, was asked once what the secret of his Christian life was. He replied: 'There came a day when I resolved that God would have everything there is of William Booth'. Many years later when his daughter was reminded of his words, she responded: 'There is a sense in which that is not the whole truth. The whole truth is that *he kept his promise*'.

(ii) *Daniel made his stand at the beginning of his life as an exile in Babylon.* This was one of the things which distinguished him from many of his contemporaries who had enjoyed similar privileges in earlier life. We discover in Psalm 137 that it was not long before a rather sad note entered into their lives. By the waters of Babylon they were taunted by their captors: 'Sing us one of the songs of Zion'. Their response was: 'How can we sing the Lord's song in a strange land?' Why was this? They had refused to pay the price of standing up before men as the Lord's servants. Now they found that any desire they had once had to please God and honour him had been eaten away.

How different Daniel was! He could sing the Lord's song in a strange land, and he did so without shame. All knew whose he was and whom he served! From the beginning he resolved to shine for his God.

Had Daniel failed here, it is likely that he would

have failed again. One battle is not the whole war. But when we have to fight succeeding battles with the same resources which were previously defeated, we stand less chance of success. That is why the initial moral victory was so important.

If you would grow in grace you must fly the flag of Christ. You must do so on the first opportunity. Otherwise there will be much lost ground to be recovered—in some cases too much. Whenever you find yourself in a new and strange situation, whether it be a new class at school or college, a new sports team or club, a new neighbourhood or job, Dare to be a Daniel! You will not need to go out of the way to seek opportunities to take your stand for Christ and his word. They will come; do not force them, or artificially provoke others. Begin as you mean to continue, and you will continue.

(iii) *Daniel's victory in his first test was the preparation for a series of later tests.* Had he failed here it is unlikely that he would have proved such a magnificent witness in later years of his life. This is why Paul tells us to make the most of every opportunity, because the days are evil (Eph. 5:16). In Daniel 4, 5 and 6 we read of the tremendous tests through which he came under the reigns of Nebuchadnezzar, Belshazzar and Darius. Because the foundations of his life had been properly dug in wholehearted consecration, it was able to take the many strains he later faced. Sure foundations mean lasting stability. Weak foundations mean a suspect testimony, and perhaps a life which will never really show the fruits of perseverance in the faith.

What, then, was Daniel's secret? It lay in the decision of his heart. He engaged his mind and will in a decisive commitment to his Lord. He 'resolved', or, more literally, 'he laid it on his heart' that he would live in a certain way. He took the principle of wholehearted allegiance to God and to his word as though it were a weight. He placed that weight solemnly and deliberately on his conscience. He bound himself by a personal covenant with God to live for his glory.

We do that far too infrequently today. We fail to devote ourselves deliberately to the Lord. But if we are ever to make progress in Christian living to any marked degree, few things are more important.

When did you last make such a resolution? Does that explain the present standard of your Christian living?

WITHSTANDING OPPOSITION

Daniel's resolution to serve God wholeheartedly was soon put to the test. The opening chapter of his story records a series of incidents which were deliberately planned in order to destroy spiritual growth in his and his companions' lives. Reading between the lines we can see that the powers of darkness were determined to spoil the quality of this young believer's life before it in turn made inroads into their monopoly in the kingdom of Babylon.

The devil has no new tricks. That is one of the most obvious lessons we learn from his attacks on Daniel. Paul said that 'we are not unaware of his schemes' (2 Cor. 2:11). That will be true if we pay careful attention to the pattern of his working in the lives recorded in Scripture. We may anticipate his activity in our lives by recognising his presence in the temptations described and analysed in the pages of Scripture.

The first onslaught on Daniel and his faithful friends was intended to bring confusion into their thinking. They were given new names. These four young men had been given specifically Jewish names by their parents. Nor were these merely names of national significance. They provided (and were intended to convey) religious and spiritual encouragement.

Daniel means *God has judged.* He was to be called Belteshazzar, meaning *May Bel protect.* Hannaniah means *God has been gracious,* but he became known as Shadrach, meaning *Command of Aku.* Mishael's name, which signified *Who is what God is?* was subtly altered to Meshach which means *Who is what Aku is?* Azariah means *God has helped,* but the name he was given in Babylon, Abednego means *Servant of Nebo.* Bel, Aku and Nebo were, of course, Babylonian deities.

The point of this name change should not be ignored. It was not simply a triviality. Nor was it merely a harmless case of 'When in Rome do as the Romans do'. Its intention and its potential consequences were far reaching. So far reaching that, had this exercise fulfilled its function in the lives of these youngsters the book of Daniel would never have been written. There would be no tales of heroic faith to pass on to successive generations. There would be no example to hold up before ourselves at all.

The menace of these new names was their intention to erode the distinctive testimony of God's servants; to provide subtle ways of saying to them: 'Now that you are in Babylon, settle into a new life-style. Forget that you belong to Jehovah God. Forget that he is judge (Daniel), that he has been gracious (Hannaniah), that he is incomparable (Mishael) and that he has been your helper (Azariah). One god is as good as another. Distinctive, costly love for the living and true God is of no consequence. Indeed it is a positive disadvantage here. *Forget about being different.* This was the temptation.

Does the devil speak any differently today? How easily he seems to be able to get us to run from one extreme to the other. For a time our immaturity will take us into an over restrictive life-style which finds no place in the teaching of Scripture. But then (as is surely the case among evangelicals today) we err just as seriously by seeming to give the impression that there is really nothing very different after all about being a Christian. In either case we have been overtaken by one of the devil's oldest tricks. He chooses his times to lead Christians into eroding the difference between faith and unbelief, the life of God and the ways of this world. 'People will think you are strange, unattractive, peculiar, if you show how different a Christian really is. So, show them that you are no different. Show them (to use a popular phrase in evangelical testimony) that "you can be a Christian and enjoy yourself just the same way everybody else does"'. How we reduce the power of the gospel in our lives when we begin to think like that! For, in essence, we have already capitulated. We are already thinking that it is far more important how the world thinks of us (or how we think of ourselves) than that we live for God and his glory and allow *him* to look after our reputations among our fellows.

This was exactly the kind of false thinking into which the Babylonians were attempting to lead Daniel and his companions. They recognised the temptation, fought against its tendencies, and proved that being different for the sake of the Lord is the most attractive way we can possibly live. It is also the only way really to grow.

The second onslaught was intended to indoctrinate their minds, so that their grasp of God's truth was weakened. They were educated for a period of three years in the 'language and literature of the Babylonians' (Dan. 1:4).

What was the point of this exercise? It was gradually to wear away the basic thought patterns, the appreciation of God's truth and the practical application of his word which were the chief elements in the education they would have already received. Imperceptible destruction often proves to be the most successful. The sluggard who lies in bed for a 'little more sleep' discovers that he eventually becomes incapable of activity and is overtaken by disaster (Prov. 6:9–11; 24:33–4). So the process of ungodly indoctrination (which surrounds us daily in the western world) erodes our sense of commitment to Christ, our ability to detect the difference between what is good, indifferent and bad. Just as men climb mountains 'because they are there', so we learn to accept standards in our own hearts, practices in our lives, attitudes and dispositions, simply because they are part of the world in which we live.

It is not difficult to test where we stand here. All we need to do is to place our actual practice of the Christian life beside some of the demanding moral exhortations of Scripture. Can we read through the moral application of the gospel (which we find so often in the second part of Paul's letters, or in the application of the Sermon on the Mount) without a sense of concern that the sharp edge of our testimony to Christ has been blunted? Do we allow our eyes to look at things we would have shunned in less permissive days in society in general? Are we numbed by what we see in the media, so that we no longer turn away eye and heart and mind from what will eventually destroy our moral fibre? I remember hearing of a prayer meeting (reputedly held in Northern Ireland!) at which one man was heard to begin his prayer in the following mildly sarcastic terms: 'Lord, you know that all of us here present are evangelicals; every single one of us. But, O Lord, you know that we've put all the emphasis on the "jelly"'. Perhaps we find the humour unfortunate. But the sentiment is too close for comfort. We can so easily degenerate into being 'jelly-fish' Christians, lacking a central nervous system, with no backbone for moral and spiritual distinctiveness. Jellyfish are at the mercy of the tide.

Satan was out to destroy these young potential leaders of the cause of God. Indoctrination was his second weapon.

The third onslaught was intended to dull their appetite for spiritual reality. Food and wine were provided for them 'from the king's table' (Dan. 1:5). It was this, as we have already seen, which proved to be the crunch issue for Daniel. He knew, besides the question of this food being dedicated to false idols, that the king's aim was to give these Hebrew teenagers a taste for pleasure in order to spoil their usefulness.

Few young men have more earned the right to speak about this than young Robert Murray M'Cheyne, whose outstanding work as an evangelist and preacher was cut short at the age of twenty-nine. Speaking during the course of a

friend's ordination, he addressed him personally
in words we do well to take to heart:

> Study universal holiness of life! Your whole
> usefulness depends on this. Your sermon
> . . . lasts but an hour or two,—your life
> preaches all the week. Remember, ministers are
> standard-bearers. Satan aims his fiery darts at
> them. *If he can only make you a covetous
> minister, or a lover of pleasure, or a lover of
> praise, or a lover of good eating, then he has
> ruined your ministry for ever.* Ah! let him
> preach on fifty years, he will never do me any
> harm. Dear brother, cast yourself at the feet of
> Christ, implore his Spirit to make you a holy
> man.

Nor is there one standard of purity and consecration in the Christian life for ministers and
another for everyone else!

Resolve to let nothing dull your palate. Let
nothing spoil your appetite for the service of God
and his kingdom.

> *From subtle love of softening things,*
> *From easy choices, weakenings,*
> *Not thus are spirits fortified,*
> *Not this way went the crucified,*
> *From all that dims Thy Calvary,*
> *O Lamb of God, deliver me.*
>
> Amy Carmichael

DISCIPLINED SPIRITUALITY

One of the impressive things about Daniel's life is
that he kept on being faithful. He not only began

well, as we have seen, but he continued to grow spiritually throughout his life.

An amazing illustration of this appears in chapters 9 and 10. Daniel had been a young teenager when the exile began. These chapters record some of his experiences when it was almost at an end. For seventy years he had been singing 'the Lord's song in a strange land'. Now, in his eighties, he was studying God's word, devoting many hours to the work of prayer and intercession, and even continuing to fast. When all his contemporaries from his days as a leading civil servant in Babylon were spending their last days 'enjoying themselves' in the Hanging Gardens of Babylon, Daniel was still showing the same spirit of the spiritual warrior he had been all his life. How wonderful! He was a living proof of the words of the psalmist:

The righteous will flourish like a palm tree,
    they will grow like a cedar of Lebanon;
planted in the house of the Lord,
    they will flourish in the courts of our God.
They will still bear fruit in old age,
    they will stay fresh and green,
proclaiming, 'The Lord is upright;
    he is my Rock, and there is no wickedness in
    him.'

Psalm 92:12–15

What were the evidences in his life that he grew steadily through the years? What were the major compass points which gave his life such clear direction. Again we can select only a few of the most outstanding ones for special mention.

(i) *Daniel was a man of prayer*. His whole life was prayer; he had learned that knowing God means learning to live always in his presence. What Jesus was later to teach as a basic aspect of the Christian life—living before the face of our Father (Matt. 6:1ff)—Daniel experienced. Prayer was his instinctive reaction to every situation.

But there is a reason why he grew into this intimate communion with God. He made prayer a discipline, a habit, a regular exercise in his life. Notice the times at which we are told he prayed. He prayed with his three closest friends in a time of crisis recorded in Daniel 2. Nebuchadnezzar's megalomania had affected him to the extent that he was demanding the impossible of his court intellectuals. He had experienced a disturbing dream. He wanted his advisers to tell him both what the dream had been and what its meaning was! He threatened them with their lives. Daniel and his companions' lives were in danger. They prayed that their testimony to God's name would not be destroyed. God heard their prayer and gave Daniel supernatural insight. *Daniel was a man who believed in corporate prayer.* He saw that he himself needed corporate prayer, and he urged his friends to pray with him (Dan. 2:18).

He was also a man who prayed privately. We read about him in later life praying on his own (Dan. 9) as well as with others (Dan. 10:7). The outstanding example of this is the insight we are given in Daniel 6 into his regular habit of prayer. Despite the ruling of the king, Daniel 'went home to his upstairs room where the windows opened toward Jerusalem. Three times a day he got down on his knees and prayed, giving thanks to his God, just as he had done before' (Dan. 6:10).

Regular, disciplined times of prayer were spiritual exercises which used to be urged upon all Christians as part and parcel of the Christian life. In many Christian groups today that is no longer true. Regular praying is regarded as something of an irksome duty, a bondage. It smacks of 'legalism'.

There is no doubt that it is possible to be legalistic about prayer. The Pharisees, or many of them, were obviously legalistic. But could we say Daniel was? Very often the truth of the matter, when people speak about regular prayer as bondage, is that *it would* be bondage *for them*. Indeed, any serious spiritual discipline would be bondage for them. But is that not an indication of how far our hearts are from enjoying the love of God?

We make the great mistake of putting the cart before the horse. Our thinking is: I will pray if I feel like praying. Then, when I feel more like praying perhaps I will pray with greater regularity. But that is not the pattern of biblical experience. Daniel prayed regularly, individually and with others. It was out of that discipline that his life of prayer developed. You do not become a master musician by playing just as you please, by imagining that learning the scales is just sheer legalism and bondage! No, true freedom in any area of life is the consequence of regular discipline. It is no less true of the life of prayer.

(ii) *Daniel was a student of God's word*. It was God's word which had first led him to the conviction that to share in the king's food would be to mar his fellowship with God. Again, whenever Daniel prays or speaks in the narrative of his life we are left with the impression of a man whose mind is saturated in the thinking of the rest of the Old Testament. His worship of God in Daniel 2 is reminiscent of the praise of that other figure of unusual spiritual appreciation beyond her years,

Mary the mother of Jesus (Lk. 1:46ff). His whole soul seems to be enlarged with a spirit of worship:

> He changes times and seasons;
>   he sets up kings and deposes them.
> He gives wisdom to the wise
>   and knowledge to the discerning.
> He reveals deep and hidden things;
>   he knows what lies in darkness,
>   and light dwells with him.
> I thank and praise you, O God of my fathers . . .
>   Daniel 2:20–23

But once more the most fascinating scene is towards the end of his life. He is now at least eighty years of age. We find him digging into God's word still, and discovering fresh light breaking out from it! In the first year of Darius he was reading the book of Jeremiah (Dan. 9:2). We know exactly which passages he must have been studying—Jeremiah 25:11–12 and 29:10. It dawned on him what these words meant: Soon the exile would be over and the people of God would be able to return home! Yet there was no sign Daniel could see which could be understood as a forerunner of the promise of God being fulfilled. That is why Daniel 9 records his pleading with God to be faithful to his word, as he had always been in Daniel's own experience.

When we cease to feed on God's word like this, to have our eyes opened to discover wonderful things in it (Ps. 119:18), we have stopped growing as Christians. Naturally there will be days (and passages of Scripture) which do not yield as much as others. But not to continue to be learning—this is a serious condition.

'Like newborn babes' says Peter, 'crave pure

spiritual milk, so that by it you may grow up in your salvation, now that you have tasted that the Lord is good' (1 Pet. 2:2). Those last words form an interesting foundation for his exhortation to go on growing. They exactly express one further element which was essential to Daniel's continued progress in the faith.

TRUST IN GOD'S GOODNESS

We frequently use the expression 'growing in grace'. We do not always appreciate that it means growing in *grace*, that is, the free and full love of God even for sinners. For there is little doubt that often the ultimate stumbling block to growth in Christians' lives is their inability to grasp the wealth of love and care which God lavishes upon them. It does not penetrate to us that God loves us, or, on the other hand, we do not appreciate that grace is given to us to produce lives of gratitude to him.

This feature of spiritual experience is illustrated unexpectedly in one of the last parables of our Lord's ministry. He pictured the time between his work on earth and his return in power in terms of a Lord leaving his servants in charge of his affairs while he himself went on a long journey. The servants were given quite different gifts and responsibilities. But each one was expected to take what he was given and develop it. One man failed to do this. The reason he gave to his Lord when he returned was: 'Master, *I knew that you are a hard man* . . . So I was afraid and went out and hid your talent in the ground. See here is what belongs to you' (Matt. 25:25).

The point should not be missed. A wrong view

of God leads inevitably to a failure to enjoy and grow in his grace. Failure to appreciate his love, his kindness and generous heart leads eventually to a life which bears no fruit and makes no true and lasting progress. The lesson is clear: if you would grow in grace, learn what grace is. Taste and see that the Lord is good.

Daniel saw this. His prayers demonstrate his appreciation of God's care for him. But nowhere is his understanding so clear as in the opening words of his great prayer in Daniel 9:

> O Lord, the great and awesome God, who keeps his covenant of love with all who love him and obey his commands . . .
>
> Daniel 9:4

He saw that God's love is the most awesome thing about him. It is not his justice, nor his majesty, not even his blazing holiness, but the fact that he has made and keeps a covenant of personal commitment and love to his people.

Daniel only had glimpses of what this implied. He knew about the rock cut without human hands which would destroy the kingdoms of this world and grow to become a huge mountain which would fill the whole earth (Dan. 2:31–5). He knew of 'one like a Son of Man' who would come with the clouds of heaven to receive authority, glory and sovereign power (Dan. 7:13). What he could not fully appreciate was that God would prove his love to us in that while we were still sinners Christ died for us (Rom. 5:8). He saw only a faint outline what we have come to know in reality— the full measure of grace. Yet what he did know made him faint with sheer wonder. He was a man who spent the whole of his life amazed by grace.

Such a spirit is the perfect seed bed for true spiritual growth.

Are there any of these signs of growth in your life?

9: Simon Peter—Fits and Starts

It is difficult to imagine many biblical characters less like Daniel than Simon Peter was.

The whole shape of Peter's personality, the case of his mind, the spirit which drove him on through life were all at the opposite end of the spectrum from what we imagine Daniel must have been. While Daniel stood firm under pressure, Peter always seemed to crack. While we see in Daniel's life a vivid illustration of the fact that

> *Each vict'ry will help you*
> *Some other to win*

in the case of Peter the very reverse is demonstrated. His failure at one stage in his life seems to have virtually guaranteed his lack of success at later stages of his experience.

Peter failed often during the period of his membership of the small band of disciples who faithfully followed Jesus during his ministry. He failed most obviously at the end of that period, when he denied his Master. But events took place which changed his life. He became a new and different man in Christ. He became a 'rock' according to his Lord's promise. Yet, even after the great events of Christ's death, resurrection and ascension, indeed even after the Day of Pentecost when Peter received an unusual filling with the Holy Spirit, he failed.

Paul narrates the sad story:

When Peter came to Antioch, I opposed him to his face, because he was in the wrong. Before certain men came from James, he used to eat with the Gentiles. But when they arrived, he began to draw back and separate himself from the Gentiles because he was afraid of those who belonged to the circumcision group. The other Jews joined him in his hypocrisy, so that by their hypocrisy even Barnabas was led astray.

When I saw that they were not acting in line with the truth of the gospel, I said to Peter in front of them all, "You are a Jew, yet you live like a Gentile and not like a Jew. How is it, then, that you force Gentiles to follow Jewish customs?

Galatians 2:11–14

What had happened was this. God had clearly shown Peter that the gospel message was to be brought to the Gentiles (See Acts 10–11). Peter had learned that in Christ the old distinctions between Jew and Gentile had been abolished (cf. Eph. 2:11–21). The rites which formerly separated them had been fulfilled in the work of Christ. They had been but symbols and shadows of what he would do. Now that Christ had appeared those symbols were no longer necessary.

When Peter had grasped this it brought not only a new conviction about doctrine to him, but also revolutionised his way of life. Now he need feel no qualms about eating with Gentiles! He was free to enjoy table fellowship with them. His conscience, which had once been bound to such a restrictive practice (contrary to God's original intention for his people) had now been set free by God's word. Like Martin Luther after him, Peter's conscience was led captive to the word of God. But that captivity is perfect freedom.

Then something snapped. Some of the 'old guard' arrived on the scene. Instead of fixing his conscience on what God had shown him, Peter allowed it to become captive to the opinions of men. He conformed to the kind of conduct which would keep him in good standing with those Paul describes as 'the circumcision party' (those who insisted that Jewish observances had to be added to what Christ had done in order to experience full salvation).

Paul had the courage to confront Peter about this. He did not accuse him of failing to understand the gospel. Peter's failure was not really intellectual, for he had understood perfectly what the implications of the gospel were. The trouble was, as Paul saw that Peter and the others 'were not acting in line with the truth of the gospel' (Gal. 2:14). Indeed Paul accused Peter of *moral* failure. Fear (v. 12) and hypocrisy (v. 13) were the charges of which he was guilty. He was proving to be a double minded man with two standards fighting for supremacy in his heart—what *God* said and what *men* said. He was guilty of hypocrisy, because knowing that what God had said was true, he was living by the standards of men. He was guilty too of fear. *That is significant because fear was his old enemy.* Jesus had spoken to Peter about it before, from the very beginning of his discipleship (Lk. 5:10; 12:5ff). It was fear that had led to Peter's denial of his Master on the eve of the crucifixion. Now Paul's diagnosis was that the old complaint had returned. Peter's Achilles' heel was exposed and wounded once again.

This sad occasion in Simon Peter's life is very instructive for us today. The fact of the matter is that Christians are always liable to claim either too much or too little for the Christian life—never more so than today. This experience in the story of a great and ultimately faithful apostle should safeguard us from both of those mistakes. For Peter was growing in grace *despite this failure*. Moreover, although he was growing in grace— and had been mightily baptised with the Spirit on the Day of Pentecost—*no crisis in his life provided a guarantee against future failure*. God sends crises into the life of his child generally speaking to remove blockages and to make true growth possible. That was what was happening in Peter's life. But no crisis rendered him immune to future failure.

What are the general lessons we can learn then about spiritual growth from these considerations? We have already indicated that no special blessing we receive guarantees automatic progress. But there are several other significant insights which we should notice:

1. Spiritual growth is not the same in every Christian. It is not possible neatly to package the ways in which God brings us on to maturity and then suggest that everyone must fit in to this pattern. That would be foolish, and it would also be very unbiblical.

Peter's life was punctuated by a series of crises which God used to restore him and to lead him past hurdles in his life which otherwise would have been insurmountable. The 'Daniel Treatment' (if we can call it that) would have been fruitless in Peter's case. Just so the 'Peter Treatment' may not be God's pattern of operating in your life. We ought to submit to whatever pattern God uses; to learn from the variety of illustration in the Bible that he has many patterns. Peter himself liked to speak about 'the multi-coloured grace of God' (1 Pet. 4:10), and in his own spiritual growth we see one of the patterns which that grace creates in a Christian's life.

2. Another important lesson we can learn from Peter is that growth can take place despite failure. Indeed, in his case growth continued despite *repeated* failure.

We often make the mistake of confusing *growth* with *perfection*. But no spiritual development in this life is without its weaknesses. Peter's failures were contained within the purposes of God for his life; they were not outside of God's control. They could not destroy what God intended to do with his life. None the less, his failures were real and provided a barrier to his development. So long as he continued in them he would never develop that stability and assurance which he needed. Perhaps it was this which led him to reflect on the fact that the Christian is 'kept by the power of God'. But he recognised this was 'through faith' (1 Pet. 1:5).

3. The third thing we should notice in general is that Peter's life was haunted by one particular failure. There was a specific weakness in his character which Satan seemed to be able to break down with alarming regularity. Peter is not alone among biblical characters in this regard. David showed distinctly similar symptoms in a very different area, as did Samson and Solomon before and after him. They had to learn through bitter experience that we must guard our weaknesses. Growth in grace sometimes depends on the relatively mundane expedient of knowing ourselves

well enough to recognise what are the points of lowest resistance in our lives.

Peter's great weakness was his fear—fear of suffering and fear of men. We have already suggested that the only remedy for such fear is the true fear of God. Several times in his letters Peter himself makes reference to the fear of God. Clearly by the end of his life he had experienced the truth of what Jesus had said. Very often it is only the fear of God which is able to bring such deliverance as this, and to lead us on past our failures to a new stability and strength in our walk with God.

4. Peter's life also teaches us not to measure spiritual growth by outward appearances and standards. To do so is to forget that God looks on the heart. But it is also to forget something else. For spiritual growth can only be measured against the unique factors which exist in every single Christian's life. It frequently involves not only outward and real expressions of the fruit of the Spirit, *but also the amount of opposition which has been overcome in order to produce such fruit.*

This is why some Christians appear to go on in their spiritual pilgrimage by leaps and bounds, others by fits and starts, and yet others almost imperceptibly. Spiritual growth is like an iceberg—only part of it can ever be seen above the surface. Someone whose life manifests only small degrees of love, joy, peace, longsuffering and all the other virtues of the work of the Spirit may in fact have grown tremendously in grace even to reach that apparently small measure of maturity. So it was with Simon Peter. His glaring failures tend to divert attention from the fact that, despite much natural opposition; despite the special, concentrated opposition of Satan towards him, he did grow spiritually. It is a possible (and perhaps a likely) interpretation of Jesus' words 'Satan has demanded to have you, Peter, to sift you like wheat' (Lk. 22:21) that Peter knew more opposition from Satan than any of the other disciples. He had been singled out for an all-out attack because of his strategic position in the disciple band and there-after in the early church. Do not be discouraged by slow progress against great opposition. Remember that progress includes opposition overcome as well as outward evidences of grace.

So much for these general lessons which arise out of Peter's life. We must now give more direct attention to some of the stages in his experience which were strategic points, indeed perhaps crisis points in his pilgrimage. His life was full of such moments, but there are one or two which seem to have become important landmarks in his life.

THE PROMISE OF GROWTH

When Jesus was first introduced to Simon he said to him: 'You are Simon son of John. You will be called Cephas" (which, when translated, is Peter)' (Jn. 1:42). The giving of a name (actually what we would call a 'nickname') in this way was an extremely significant thing—just as it still is today. Often we learn much more about people by their nicknames than we do from their proper names! Peter was to be called 'Rocky' (the nearest modern equivalent despite its obvious Americanism). Perhaps that conjures up memories of the famous heavyweight boxer 'Rocky' Marciano, if you belong to the appropriate generation. Peter was to be the heavyweight champion of the disciples. We always imagine him as such—big, blustering, impatient, determined, swinging alternate uppercuts and left hooks at his opponents, only to be knocked down and almost counted out by a skilled blow from his adversary the Devil.

Jesus did not give Simon his new name without appreciating that there was a touch of irony in it. But he also intended that it should express what would, ultimately, be the truth about his disciple. He would be a rock. He would become steady, reliable, a landmark to friends and foes of the gospel. 'You are . . . you will be'. The contrast summarised all that Jesus intended to do to bring him to maturity.

What lesson are we meant to learn from this? This: Peter's life can only be properly understood as the transformation of a man from what he was into what Christ intended him to be. It cannot properly be interpreted if we take into consideration only what he was; nor if we concentrate only on what he was to become. For many of the incidents in his life make plain that he was being moulded out of one life-style into another. The man he was during that process is often either inexplicable or simply disappointing. The experiences through which he passed, when isolated and interpreted without reference to Christ's ultimate goal, give us a very depressing view of his advance in the Christian life. Only when we see the finished product, the aim in view, are we able to understand the pattern by which Peter was being moulded. Only when we remember that Christ was making a rock out of him can we appreciate why all the hammer blows he experienced were so very necessary. In his own words, his faith was impure. In order to become purified like gold it had to be refined in the fire (1 Pet. 1:7).

It was Paul who most eloquently enunciated this principle, but it might well have been Peter:

> We rejoice in the hope of the glory of God. Not only so, but we also rejoice in our sufferings, because we know that suffering produces perseverance; perseverance, character; and character, hope.
>
> Romans 5:2–4

God had used the same process centuries before in the life of the impetuous Moses. As a young man he seems to have assumed that he could become the deliverer of the Israelites in a day. But God took forty years of his life to prepare and equip him for the work of the Exodus. He taught him patience through exile, just as he taught Paul grace through sufferings (2 Cor. 12:9).

In each test Peter experienced; each trial through which he came often feeling a total failure, Christ was strengthening him, building solid and lasting foundations into his character. Like his Lord, Peter became mature through his suffering. Maturity was the necessary qualification for his ministry. It is perhaps not without significance that it was only after he had denied Christ and was restored that he was ordained to the work of pastoring the flock as well as evangelising the lost (Jn. 21:15–17).

DISCOVERING PERSONAL SINFULNESS

In the narrative of Luke's Gospel the call of Simon to discipleship is given with greater detail than elsewhere. Luke tells of the miraculous catch of fish after the fruitless night of fishing which had preceded the young fisherman's dramatic encounter with Jesus. Peter, in the process of being called to follow Christ as a 'fisher of men' appears to have come to a sudden and profound consciousness of his personal sinfulness and unworthiness. He fell down before Jesus and said: 'Go away from me, Lord; I am a sinful man!' (Lk. 5:8)

What happened to Peter? He had become conscious of the power and majesty of Jesus. The effect of this was dramatic. For Peter this was an hour of unusual self-understanding. Any illusions he entertained about himself were demolished in the presence of Christ. All he could say when confronted by him was 'I have sinned'.

We have no means of knowing what Peter's 'self image' as we now call it might have been. At one time it seems he was a disciple or adherent of John the Baptist. Undoubtedly John's preaching had a solemnising influence on his life. Perhaps it had made him endeavour to bring forth fruits meet for repentance (Lk. 3:8). But somehow this encounter was different. Peter did not yet fully understand who Christ was; but he understood more fully who he himself was. He felt himself exposed, his personality and sinfulness dismantled before the presence of this Jesus. Whatever self-image he had—and presumably we find him returning to it from time to time in the rest of his life—his illusions received a mortal blow. Now, in a sense, he did not know what to make of himself. All he knew was that he was a sinner.

Under such circumstances the Lord Jesus

called Simon to be his disciple. He promised to make something quite new out of the life which was offered to him. He was Simon, he would become Peter; he was a fisherman, and now he would become a fisher of men. The most radical reconstruction of his life had begun. But it had to begin by demolishing the manner in which Peter had previously thought of himself.

None of the other disciples experienced their call in the same dramatic way, as far as we know. Peter's experience on its own is not enough for us to make a general principle out of his conviction of sin. Not all people need the same sight of their own sinfulness to bring them to Christ. But often a deep sense of sin and guilt, such as Peter was given, has a very definite purpose. God does not humble us, or humiliate us without a special reason. In Peter's case his self-image was a definite hindrance to God's plan to lead him to a life of Christ-likeness.

Again it is important to notice that while this is not an invariable rule of God's dealings with us, bringing a deep consciousness of personal sin is a pattern which he often weaves into the lives of those whom he intends to use in a special way.

Isaiah the prophet is perhaps the clearest illustration of this in the Old Testament. He may already have served God officially in the prophetic ministry. But then God broke into his life in unusual power. He had already preached that the people had unclean lips, but now his self image was shattered by the discovery of something to which he had doubtless paid lip service before: 'I am a man of unclean lips' (Is. 6:5). He saw the King, the Lord Almighty; he saw the Son of God, the Christ (according to Jn. 12:41). He experienced what Peter experienced.

What is God doing to us through experiences which have this effect on us? They may come when God speaks to us through his word, or through some event which breaks our hearts. On such occasions of spiritual crisis God is rebuilding solid foundations for the rest of our Christian lives. He is digging further down into the secret and sometimes confused and weak recesses of our hearts, in order to form something new and lasting at the very heart of our lives. To change the metaphor, he is root-pruning, so that everything that impairs our spiritual growth (but might otherwise remain undetected) can be properly dealt with.

Jeremiah expressed this same thought about his own ministry, and it is significant that God built it into the original call he gave him to be a prophet: 'See, today I appoint you over nations and kingdoms to uproot and tear down, to destroy and overthrow, to build and to plant' (Jer. 1:10). It is not surprising that when Martin Luther wrote his commentary on the Letter to the Romans (which had meant so much to him in his own spiritual experience as 'the clearest gospel of them all'), he used these words of Jeremiah to describe what its teaching does in men's lives. It plucks up and roots out—and then plants the strong grace of God in our hearts.

There can be few more alarming sights than the sight of what we would be were we left to ourselves; of what we are by nature in and of ourselves. It is a sight which few of us are able to bear for any length of time. That is why such experiences are usually brief, pointed and not prolonged. God gives us enough to make us see our need, to break down any illusions we may have had about ourselves. Like a skilled surgeon his knife work is fast, accurate and clean. Like a skilled surgeon also, the Lord knew that Simon Peter would need similar treatment again. At a later stage of his life he would need the most serious treatment consistent with the maintenance of his spiritual life. But when he fell on his knees before Jesus the treatment had begun. He could never really be the same again.

THE CRISIS OF THE CROSS

What was the real issue involved in the spiritual development of Peter? Unhesitatingly we can say that, throughout his life, he had a tendency to draw back from the cross and its implications. Even in the circumstances which Paul describes in Galatians, when Peter feared the men who emphasised the need for circumcision and the continuation of the old religious rites, this was the issue which underlay his fears. Paul said that he was not living in a way that was consistent with the gospel. There was an unwillingness to express the heart of the gospel in his manner of life. But that had always been a weakness in Peter's Christian life, and a hurdle at which he had frequently stumbled and fallen.

It was after Peter's confession of Jesus as the Christ, the Son of God (Mk. 8:27ff) that Jesus 'then began to teach them that the Son of Man must suffer many things and be rejected by the elders, chief priests and teachers of the law, and that he must be killed . . .' (Mk. 8:31). Peter immediately 'took him aside and began to rebuke him' (Mk. 8:32). What a remarkable scene! Peter's response to our Lord's first plain declaration of his purpose to die on the cross was one of hostility and rejection. What he did not realise was that he had already played his life into Satan's hands (hence Jesus' words of counter-rebuke 'Get out of my sight, Satan'). Peter was merely echoing the voice Jesus had already heard in the wilderness temptations, enticing him to take some other, less sacrificial way to win the world.

Yet Peter's experience is but a dramatic illustration of a crisis which faces all of us. He wanted the salvation which the Messiah would bring; but he was little prepared for its implications—either for Jesus or for himself. He did not yet understand the necessity of the cross (which we considered in chapter four); but he did seem to grasp (as so many people instinctively do) what its implications would be for himself. Jesus' crucifixion entailed a parallel sacrifice in the lives of his disciples. It meant taking up the cross daily to follow him (Lk. 9:23). Being a Christian would therefore imply following a crucified, humiliated, rejected Messiah, whose triumph and victory could be seen only by faith.

Peter's refusals of this central feature of his Master's life followed thereafter at regular intervals: in his instinctive recoil from the thought that Jesus should humiliate himself by washing his disciples' feet (Jn. 13:1ff); in his unwillingness to openly confess that he was his follower; in his later compromise for which Paul (following Jesus) rebuked him. There was always a tendency to return to the old pattern of a life which avoided sharing in the crucifixion of Christ.

This is not to suggest that no advance was made. The reverse is in fact the truth. Peter experienced something very profound on the eve of the crucifixion when he went out and wept bitterly. He experienced Christ's incisive pastoral dealings when he was later restored during that painful interview by the Sea of Galilee (Jn. 21:15ff). The new foundations which Jesus was laying in his life then were the prelude to what would take place in Peter's life on the Day of Pentecost, when he was so mightily filled with the Spirit.

THE PATTERN

Peter grew in grace. It is tempting to think that what made the difference was either or both of the events to which his new life is generally attributed. A common interpretation of his experience suggests that he was changed by the fact that Christ had risen. A second view suggests that he was changed by the events of the Day of Pentecost.

Clearly it was not just the resurrection which changed Peter. There were still fears, still some of the old impetuous tendencies apparent even after the resurrection (Jn. 20:19; 21:7). Nor would it be accurate to separate off what happened at Pentecost and suggest that there lies the key to his spiritual development. The fact of the matter is that both of these events, and their powerful influence on Peter's life were dependent on the crucifixion and death of Jesus. It alone gives them significance, just as we need them in order to see the real purpose of our Lord's death. That is reflected in Peter's life. Only by at last yielding his life to a *crucified* Saviour was he able to receive the power of the Holy Spirit at Pentecost. Indeed, the real preparation of Peter for Pentecost had begun the day that Jesus first explained the necessity of the cross.

There is in fact a good deal of evidence that this is how Peter himself viewed these events. We do not find him speaking about Pentecost as the event which gives shape and power to the life of the Christian. No, it is the death and resurrection of Jesus which form for him the key points. It is Peter who takes up Jesus' emphasis on his life as embodying the ministry of the Suffering Servant of Isaiah (Is. 52:13–53:12). He preaches about Jesus as the servant of God (Acts 3:13; 26 cf. 4:27, 30). In his first letter he expounds the same teaching (1 Pet. 2:21–5). The heart of the Christian life is the crucified and risen Christ; the heart of all Christian experience is fellowship with him; the key to Christian growth is by sharing in all the implications of his death and resurrection.

He began life as Simon. Jesus promised he would become Peter, a rock. As they talked together by the Sea of Galilee, Jesus explained what that would mean. Peter, who had so signally failed his Master, would, at the end of his life face the ultimate challenge:

'I tell you the truth, when you were younger you dressed yourself and went where you wanted; but when you are old you will stretch out your hands, and someone else will dress you and lead you where you do not want to go.' Jesus said this to indicate the kind of death by which Peter would glorify God. Then he said to him, 'Follow me!'

John 21:18–19

The day would come when Peter—yes, Peter!—would be willing to accept the ultimate implication of following a crucified Christ. There is possibly a reference in these words (stretch out

141

your hands) to the very way in which Peter would die.—like his Master, by crucifixion. Not only so, but Peter's death would *glorify God*. He did learn to follow Christ. He took up the cross daily. He also took up the cross finally. He had grown to the measure of the stature of the fulness of the crucified Christ. So must we. The pathway remains the same:

> *Take up thy cross, the Saviour said,*
> *If thou wouldst My disciple be;*
> *Deny thyself, the world forsake,*
> *And humbly follow after Me.*

> *Take up thy cross; let not its weight*
> *Fill thy weak soul with vain alarm;*
> *His strength shall bear thy spirit up,*
> *And brace thy heart, and nerve thine arm.*

> *Take up thy cross, nor heed the shame,*
> *Nor let thy foolish pride rebel;*
> *The Lord for thee the cross endured*
> *To save thy soul from death and hell.*

> *Take up thy cross, then, in His strength,*
> *And calmly every danger brave;*
> *'Twill guide thee to a better home,*
> *And lead to victory o'er the grave.*

> *Take up thy cross, and follow Christ,*
> *Nor think till death to lay it down;*
> *For only he who bears the cross*
> *May hope to wear the glorious crown.*
>
> Charles William Everest

10: Timothy—Coping with Yourself

The newspaper report of the Wimbledon tennis championships describes one of the most famous players as 'his own worst enemy'. Despite the large number of famous players taking part in the championship, few people would guess wrongly about his identity. It is a curious factor in every sphere of life that there always seems to be someone of whom this can be said. But in a sense it is true of all of us.

When the correspondence columns in The Times many years ago featured letters on the theme 'What is wrong with the world', the famous writer and apologist for Roman Catholicism, G. K. Chesterton contributed the shortest letter of all. It read: 'Dear Sir, I am, Yours sincerely, G. K. Chesterton'. Many of us often feel that way. But there are some Christians for whom it is true to an aggravated degree. From a psychological point of view, from the point of view of their own personality development they seem to be in a spirit of bondage, lack of assurance and insecurity which does not plague others to nearly the same extent.

Of course even a Daniel must have known an element of this. No doubt Simon Peter experienced it to a greater degree, because it feeds on failure. But another young man appears in the pages of Scripture who is immediately identified in this way as 'his own worst enemy'. Paradoxically he was also the apostle Paul's closest friend.

Paul once said that he had no friend like him (Phil. 2:20). Yet Timothy (for that was the young man's name) was plagued with fears, doubts and misgivings about the value of his Christian life and service. What he needed to learn was that the grace of God which enables us to grow as Christians works partly by giving us the help we need in order to cope with ourselves. We can discover how he did so by considering the way in which Paul offered his final pastoral counsel and encouragements to his young companion in the gospel.

TIMOTHY—YOUNG SERVANT OF CHRIST

The New Testament provides us with a number of the pieces which made the jig-saw puzzle of Timothy's life. His home was in Lystra (Acts 16:1). Although we do not know definitely when or how he became a Christian, it is probable that it was during the ministry of Paul in Lystra on his first missionary journey. On that occasion he had seen the sufferings which the apostle had experienced, and it may have been the obvious help which Christ gave him in such adversity which clinched Timothy's conversion (2 Tim 3:10–11). There seems little doubt that Paul was God's instrument in all this, because he refers affectionately to Timothy as his 'son in the faith' (1 Tim. 1:2; cf. 1:18; 2 Tim. 1:2; 2:1).

We also know that Timothy was the child of a mixed marriage. His mother Eunice was a Jewess, but his father was a Greek. Although his mother had taught him the Scriptures from his childhood—he had drunk in godliness with his mother's milk, as one commentator puts it—he had never been circumcised as a Jewish child (see Acts 16:3). Perhaps that is an indication of some of the tensions and difficulties which would have arisen in such a family.

Paul chose Timothy as one of his assistants and travelling companions. We know that his choice was sealed by a special work of the Spirit in Timothy's life (1 Tim. 4:14; 2 Tim. 1:6). His first task appears to have been to bring encouragement to the church at Thessalonica (1 Thess. 3:2). Later on he was entrusted with a mission to Corinth (1 Cor. 4:17). Paul's words to that church teach us something about it and about Timothy: 'If Timothy comes, see to it that he has nothing to fear while he is with you, for he is carrying on the work of the Lord, just as I am. No one, then, should refuse to accept him. Send him on his way in peace so that he may return to me' (1 Cor. 16:10–11). Paul obviously feared that the Corinthians might do the very reverse. He also knew how much Timothy needed to feel accepted before he could give his very best in the service of Christ.

From what we have already seen in Paul's Second Letter to the Corinthians, Timothy's mission probably accomplished little or nothing. He continued to share in Paul's ministry (Rom. 16:21; Acts 20:4, 5; Phil. 2:20 etc.). By the time Paul wrote his letters to him Timothy was his apostolic delegate and seems to have been serving for some time as the pastor of the congregation in Ephesus. Paul was, by this time, a prisoner awaiting almost certain execution. He saw that, humanly speaking, the future of the church in Ephesus lay in the hands of Timothy and his companions. He knew too that much more than the stability of one congregation might depend on Timothy's usefulness and maturity as a servant of

God. So, in Second Timothy in particular, Paul gives his final personal counsel to his dear young friend.

We know very little more about Timothy's life, except that Paul's encouragement, as we shall see, bore rich fruit.

TIMOTHY'S TRIALS

Timothy was faced with three basic problems to overcome if his spiritual growth and usefulness were not to be hindered.

Youthfulness

We know that Timothy was a young man. He may also have sometimes seemed younger than he actually was because of the nature of his looks and personality. In biblical language 'young' is an adjective which stretches a little further on in life than it does in the modern western world. Timothy may have been in his late twenties or even in his thirties when Paul wrote to him! But simply because he was a young man he faced certain problems.

Paul exhorted him to 'Flee the evil desires of youth' (2 Tim. 2:22). Clearly Timothy faced a young man's temptations, and he felt them press heavily on his life. As a leader in the congregation at Ephesus he knew that he should be a model in ruling the flock of God. In order to do that he should be able to rule himself (1 Tim. 3:2). But there lay the problem. How could he rule God's people, how could he 'encourage the young men to be self-controlled' (Tit. 2:6) when he found self-mastery a great problem in his own life?

We are all tempted. But it is noticeable in pastoral work that there are some young people who seem to be more conscious of the power of temptation than others are, who feel their weakness more and are more given to despair than their fellow Christians tend to be. There is a minor key running through their experience, a strain of melancholy which clouds even their very best moments. Such Christians very often expect to be defeated by the power of indwelling sin. Perhaps Timothy was such a Christian.

It is possible, alternatively, that Timothy had a tendency to linger when temptation was present, or that he lacked sufficient self-knowledge to avoid occasions or opportunities of temptation. In that case 'flee youthful lusts' was a much-needed exhortation.   Self-mastery is a mark of maturity in any sphere. The mastery of the sinful self is a chief mark of spiritual maturity, and it is a key to the growth of a well-rounded Christian character. What Paul was saying to Timothy to encourage him in such growth was essentially this. When we are young (in age or in grace) we tend to think that self-mastery is a relatively straightforward matter. When we are being driven along by new experiences and ambitions that is almost inevitable. Further, God seems to protect us in a remarkable way when we are young Christians; he shields us from temptation and from the many problems of the Christian life. We are able to see his grace and love so clearly that we give little attention to our own failure and sin. We see the great task in our lives as the work of evangelising those who do not yet know Christ. But soon we begin to discover that there are dimensions of experience we never knew existed; there are spiritual battles to be fought; there are sins from which we must flee. Little did Joseph think as a youngster that the day would come when the only safe thing for him to do if he was to keep on growing in grace was to run: (See Genesis ch. 39).

The situation was made more complex because Timothy was a leader. Paul had urged him not to allow his youthfulness to be abused by his fellow Christians (1 Tim. 4:12). There were so many situations for which he felt inadequate. He had so little experience. There were situations in Ephesus which Paul seemed to have coped with without special strain which kept Timothy awake at night in bed. There was opposition to the gospel which he would feel in an intensely personal way. He was also the 'curate' in the congregation of which the apostle Paul had been the 'rector': Paul had ministered there for a period of some three years, and had expounded the Scriptures for several hours each day during that period, besides his personal counselling and house-to-house visitation (Acts 20:17ff cf. 19:9–10). Timothy must have felt like a spiritual pygmy each time he tried to expound God's word to this congregation. How could he ever hope to match the teaching of the apostle?

How easy it must have been for him to become turned in on himself. And, apparently, that is what often happened. But he faced an added burden.

Constitution

Timothy was far from robust, physically. Paul reminded him: 'Stop drinking only water, and use a little wine because of your stomach and your frequent illnesses' (1 Tim. 5:23). Was this a prescription Paul had received from Dr Luke? For what ailment of the stomach? We do not know. But what we do learn from it is that Timothy was not well. Perhaps he was never really ill, but he was certainly never strong. He unquestionably would have found the weakening effect of his sickness a great burden; it was also in all likelihood a source of considerable depression.

Yet Timothy had been refusing to take wine. Perhaps, like many Christians, he had an attitude of total abstinence. Perhaps he felt that too many people in Ephesus were drunkards. Perhaps he felt that this was a real temptation to many people in the church (cf. Eph.5:18). So he abstained. He would not become enslaved to his liberties. But had he become enslaved to his denial of his liberties? Many Christians like Timothy tie themselves (and their personalities) in the tightest possible knots because they do this with all manner of things. It is a great barrier to the liberty which ought to accompany development in the Christian life. When we impose man-made regulations upon ourselves (or others) and lose sight of our liberty to do or not do those things which Scripture neither commands nor forbids, we destroy the fruit of the spirit and we cease to grow (or to allow others to grow).

Accompanying all this, and partly as a consequence of it, Timothy was a man of very shy and timid characteristics. Indeed, as far as his Christian life and service were concerned he seems to have been almost paralysed by this element in his make-up.

We have already noticed that when Paul wrote to the difficult members of the church at Corinth, he had to beg them to put Timothy at his ease. He had a 'spirit of fear' (2 Tim.1:7).

Imagine the situation today. A famous evangelist is sending a colleague to a church which bristles with problems. He writes in his letter of commendation: 'You will find that my young colleague has certain difficulties in getting to know people; he is shy and diffident. If you are going to see his work among you prove worthwhile you will need to give him great consideration. Make sure you go out of your way to welcome him and put him at his ease'. It would be interesting to be a fly on the wall of a modern congregation when this letter was read out at one of the committee meetings! How *unlike* our ideal Christian Timothy was! It is not surprising that he had a sense of inadequacy! We may well wonder if he was the product of a home dominated by his mother and grandmother (rather than his Greek father) in which he was rarely if ever given the opportunity to mould his life on a strong manly model. Be that as it may, Timothy had personal problems which were enormous obstacles to his progress in the faith.

Does this strike a chord, in our own life story and in our inner thoughts about ourselves? What was Paul's counsel? What would he say to us if we confessed that we find ourselves and our lives mirrored to some extent in the life of Timothy?

Paul's Encouragements

Paul's approach was to suggest to Timothy that his interpretation of his spiritual condition was only part of the truth. It was true that he faced all these difficulties. It was also true that on their own these would inevitably lead him to a sense of despair about his spiritual growth. But that was only half the truth, and sometimes that can be just as dangerous, spiritually, as total misunderstanding. Timothy needed to have another perspective on his life, one that was more discerning and objective than his own.

Paul gave his young friend several pieces of

encouragement. Timothy was like Mary, weeping at the tomb of Jesus, feeling that he was no longer present with her. She was so taken up with her own sense of loss that she could not recognise Jesus even when he was just beside her! Similarly, Paul could see the evident signs of the Lord's presence and influence in Timothy's life which Timothy failed to appreciate because he was looking only at his sense of failure.

Spiritual sensitivity

When Paul began to write his second letter to Timothy he allowed his mind to wander to recollect their times together in the past. How much he had appreciated Timothy's company! How easy he was to work alongside—so different from many others. Then, into Paul's mind's eye came the scene of their last meeting. Timothy had wept—openly and unashamedly as he had parted with his aged friend and father in the faith. So, wrote Paul 'I remember your tears' (2 Tim.1:4). Paul uses a word which probably means silent tears in this context. Timothy's heart had been broken open, and he could not restrain this expression of the love affection and need he felt for the apostle Paul.

What was so memorable or important about that? A very simple thing: in that moment Timothy had expressed himself fully and freely, in a manner which he had perhaps done very rarely in his life. He was taking his bottled-up emotions and pouring them out before Paul—just as the woman who washed Jesus' feet with her tears and dried them with her hair had done (Lk.7:38). Timothy, who found it so desperately difficult to give himself away to others, who was so timid and shy in self-expression, had shown in a most moving way the true spirit of brotherly love which was in his heart. It had hurt. It cost him a great deal. Perhaps afterwards he was tempted to feel ashamed of what might be misinterpreted by others as weakness. But in fact it was a gracious mark of spiritual maturity. He had crossed a growth barrier in his life.

The fruit of the Spirit is love. But love is the most costly of fruits – for reasons which C.S. Lewis finely described.

> There is no safe investment. To love at all is to be vulnerable. Love anything, and your heart will certainly be wrung and possibly be broken. If you want to make sure of keeping it intact, you must give your heart to no one, not even to an animal. Wrap it carefully round with hobbies and little luxuries; avoid all entanglements; lock it up safe in the casket or coffin of your selfishness. But in that casket—safe, dark, motionless, airless—it will change. It will not be broken; it will become unbreakable, impenetrable, irredeemable. The alternative to tragedy, or at least to the risk of tragedy, is damnation. The only place outside Heaven where you can be perfectly safe from all the dangers and perturbations of love is Hell.
>
> *The Four Loves*, pp. 111–2

Timothy had broken open the casket. He was free. Now he would grow.

Genuine Faith

The second feature Paul remembered when he thought about Timothy was his faith. At first sight that may seem a quite ordinary thing to say. But closer inspection teaches us otherwise. For how many people do you know of whom this could be said? How many Christians do you know who are associated in your mind with the presence of faith?

Paul described Timothy's faith as 'sincere' or 'genuine' or 'unfeigned' (2 Tim. 1:5). The word he uses is an extremely picturesque one—*anhupokritos*. It is simply the word 'hypocrite' with the prefix '*an*' meaning 'not'. Timothy's faith was the opposite of hypocritical.

But let us take the picture further. The hypocrite was originally an actor, a person who wore a mask on the stage. Theatrical make-up in those days took the form of a mask which the actor wore. On it would be painted the character and the mood which the actor portrayed. It might be a smiling face which hid the sad heart of the man behind it. It might be a face of virtue which hid behind it a life of vice. In acting there can be a great discrepancy between the part which is played and the reality of the life which lies behind it. Paul suggests that the same can be true of faith. We can profess much and possess little. Indeed there is always the temptation in Christian fellowships to pretend to be something other than what we are. We noticed earlier that 'truthing it in love' was one of the hallmarks of spiritual growth. So is reality in faith.

Timothy might not yet have had great faith or the full assurance of faith about which the New Testament elsewhere speaks. But he did have genuine faith. There was no double-dealing as far as he was concerned. What he seemed to be he really and truly was—a man of sincere, genuine faith.

Again Paul was reminding him of this for his encouragement. He had grown. Of course he was not all he might be. But God had room to work in his life because he was hiding nothing. Sincerity on its own is always inadequate before God. But faith without it is impossible. Timothy had both. He had begun to take solid and reliable steps towards spiritual maturity.

Spiritual powers

Paul's third line of encouragement was to say this: Look Timothy, God has equipped you to serve him in his kingdom. Do not forget the powers he has given you.

Timothy had been given a special gift. Paul exhorted him to fan it into flame (2 Tim. 1:6). But Timothy was also the recipient of the gift which every Christian receives: 'God did not give us a spirit of timidity, but a Spirit of power, of love and of self-discipline' (2 Tim. 1:7).

What is the significance of this? Paul's thinking was as follows. All our needs can be met out of the fulness of the grace, love and power of Christ. It is the Holy Spirit who brings the fulness of Christ to us. If we possess the Holy Spirit, then all that we personally need in order to grow in grace and serve Christ well is available to us.

We have already seen what were the hindrances to Timothy's spiritual growth. He was overwhelmed with a sense of his own weakness; he was by nature highly introverted; he found self-mastery one of the greatest challenges of his Christian life.

But, Paul urges: God has given you his Spirit! He is a Spirit of power, to help you in your weakness. He is a Spirit of love, to turn your life from an inward-looking to an outward-looking direction, from being concerned with your own failures to being concerned for other people's needs. God has given you the Spirit who brings self-mastery into your life! He has provided for all your needs. There was no reason on earth why Timothy should fail to keep on growing in grace.

Did he? Do we know whether Paul's words of counsel ever bore fruit? Yes, they did! Later, in the closing greetings of the Letter to the Hebrews, the writer says: 'I want you to know that our brother Timothy has been released' (Heb. 13:23). Released from what? Although the word is used in the New Testament in the sense of setting someone free for service (Acts 13:3), in this context the meaning is obvious. Timothy had been released from prison.

What is so noteworthy about these words? Were not many Christians imprisoned in those early days of the Christian church? Of course, but this is the same Timothy who had to be urged by Paul not to be ashamed of the gospel and to take his share of suffering. This was the Timothy who was so timid that he was in danger of being ashamed even of the apostle Paul's imprisonment (2 Tim. 1:8). He, Timothy, had grown so firm and strong in his life and witness that he had been willing to suffer even imprisonment for the sake of Christ. If, as we suggested earlier, spiritual growth is measured not only by external indications but by the amount of opposition which has to be overcome in order to express them—then Timothy had grown greatly in grace. Paul's encouragements and instruction had fulfilled their task.

The same word, the same grace, the same Spirit are available to us still today. Many of us and our contemporaries are like Timothy. We face great obstacles to our growth. Let us learn from his experience that they are never insurmountable.

11: Over to You

Our aim in these studies has been to try to come to grips with some of the Bible's teaching about principles of Christian growth. We have tried to do this from a number of different angles. Now we have come to the conclusion of the matter. We are like a person who has been preparing for a journey—the time comes when we must take our first steps, close the door behind us, get into the car, or boat, or train, or plane, and begin the journey in earnest. Are we ready for that?

What preparations have we made?

We began our studies by thinking about Jesus himself. If we are to grow in grace then we must aim to become more and more like him. In fact growing in grace always means growing in fellowship with Christ. But perhaps we have already discovered in our Christian lives that there seems to be opposition to this from many quarters. We are so readily taken up with ourselves and our own preoccupations with secondary matters. Or, we are caught up in the world, and we lose sight of Christ.

It is for this reason that the New Testament exhorts Christians so often to focus attention on Christ. Very many of the problems and difficulties which arose in the early church could only be solved by bringing the Christians of that time back to think about Jesus. That is why almost every letter in the New Testament has as its central theme the person and work of Jesus.

Being a Christian is knowing him; growing as a Christian means knowing him better.

Have you really taken this seriously? Are you making an effort to know Christ? He shows himself to us in many different ways, and we have thought about some of them in the preceding pages. Have you committed yourself to growing in the knowledge of Christ which inevitably accompanies growing in grace? You cannot expect to grow as long as *he* is a matter of relative indifference!

We then went on to think about what we saw to be a key principle to spiritual growth. A proper attitude for God, and a desire to get to know him better go hand-in-hand in the Christian life. We discover, perhaps to our astonishment, that fearing the Lord and longing for his presence are among the most important elements in the development of a biblical Christian life-style. Furthermore, when we turn away from these we soon discover that what we are ultimately turning from is the cross and the crucified Lord himself. If there is one thing from which the world, the flesh and the devil will together seek to draw us, it is following a crucified Saviour and being willing to accept whatever the consequences may be. We are faced therefore with a choice, as A. W. Tozer has said: We must either flee from the cross, or we must be willing to die on it. It is a challenge from which many people hide:

Perhaps this is at the bottom of the backsliding and worldliness among gospel believers today. We want to be saved but we insist that Christ do all the dying. No cross for us, no dethronement, no dying. We remain king within the little kingdon of Mansoul and wear our tinsel crown with all the pride of a Caesar; but we doom ourselves to shadows and weakness and spiritual sterility.

The Root of the Righteous, p.66.

Ever since the temptations of Christ, the devil has attempted to draw God's servants away from this central principle of Christian living and growing. But if we are to conquer him, grow in grace and become mature Christians we must accept the cross. It is as inescapable as it is radical. It is, literally, the crucial issue. Have we faced it, and decided that we shall put our hand to this plough and keep looking forward?

Then we have seen that we cannot grow in isolation. Spiritual growth means growing in love, and love can never function in a vacuum. It is with other Christians that our love and spiritual growth are both exercised and put to the test. The gifts God has given you—these have been placed in your hands so that you can reach out to touch others and their needs. You have a duty, an obligation to give what God has given you.

Are you tempted in the light of this to share your gifts only with a carefully selected group of Christians? Paul has shown us that real growth in grace means that we open our hearts to all the Lord's people. Growing as a Christian means seeking to be 'perfect' as our Father in heaven is perfect. He sends his rain on the just and the unjust alike. To whom would you send the rain, if that was your prerogative? Only to the just? Only to those who loved you?

Some of these principles and issues we have seen illustrated in the lives of Daniel, Peter and Timothy. They were all relatively young and immature believers with whom God dealt over extended periods of time. None of us is exactly like them. But most of us share some of their features. Their lives teach us that growth is not impossible, even for us! God's resources are sufficient for each of us.

Now it is up to us to work out these principles in our own lives, to put these exhortations into practise, to discern what God is doing in order to lead us on in the Christian life. Are you willing to ask God to help you to *grow in grace*?

WHY I BELIEVE

D. James Kennedy

Do you know what Christians believe, and why they believe it? Can you defend your belief against the critics all around you?

Dr. D. James Kennedy, the world renowned founder of Evangelism Explosion International, was so angry when he heard a militant atheist make mincemeat out of the Christian callers-in to a radio talk show he had to do something. From his lifetime of study he has brought together a compellingly powerful declaration of what Christians believe and why . . . intelligent, informed responses to frequently heard objections to the Christian faith.

Intensely penetrating and personal, this book is a statement you will want to make your own.

UNDER GOD'S WORD

Jim Packer

Is the Bible all true? And is it important that it should be? Jim Packer, the bestselling author of KNOWING GOD, takes a decisive stand on these questions. But he goes beyond the issue of inerrancy to the more important one of authority—what is the point of winning the battle for the Bible if in the process we lose our understanding of its role? The Bible is central to both personal and public worship. To recover truly biblical faith and practice we need to restore the Bible to its rightful place in the lives of present-day Christians and churches.

Writing with a deep pastoral concern Jim Packer brings us back to devotion and worship as the key to understanding God's word and appropriating it for ourselves. UNDER GOD'S WORD is a challenging reminder that it is nothing less than our souls which are at stake in this debate.